RELAXATION EXERCISES
FOR HORSES

RELAXATION EXERCISES FOR HORSES

A Guide to Supple, Soft, and Light

Guillaume Henry

Translated by Elizabeth Gray

Trafalgar Square
North Pomfret, Vermont

First published in the United States of America
in 2023 by
Trafalgar Square Books
North Pomfret, Vermont

Originally published in the French language as *Les Assouplissements du cheval*.

Copyright © 2022 Guillaume Henry and Éditions Vigot, 23, rue de l'École-de-Médecine, 75006 Paris, France
English translation © 2023 Trafalgar Square Books

Disclaimer of Liability
The author and publisher shall have neither liability nor responsibility to any person or entity with respect to any
loss or damage caused or alleged to be caused directly or indirectly by the information contained in this book.
While the book is as accurate as the author can make it, there may be errors, omissions, and inaccuracies.

Trafalgar Square Books encourages the use of approved riding helmets in all equestrian sports and activities.

ISBN: 978-1-64601-211-4
Library of Congress Control Number: 2023938784

Despite all the efforts of the original publisher, not all the photographers or rights holders of certain photographs in this
book could be identified or contacted. The publishers will endeavor to correct any errors or omissions in future editions.

Cover photo: Alain Laurioux
Cover illustrations: Charles Thiebaut
Photography: all photographs in this book are by Alain Laurioux,
except the following: pp 2, 18, 85, Claude Bigeon; pp 6, 10, DR
Illustrations: pp 7, 9, 11, 13, 17, 28, 31, 32, 33, 44, Marine Oussedik; pp 19, 40, 42, 45, 47, 49, 50, 52, 53, 54, 55, 57, 58, 59,
60, 67, 63, 69, 73, 74, 76, 78, 79, 80, 81, 82, 83, 84, Charles Thiebaut.

Cover design: RM Didier
Translation into English: Elizabeth Gray

Printed in China
10 9 8 7 6 5 4 3 2 1

Table of Contents

Introduction

This book presents the key principles essential to stretching, suppling, and relaxing the horse. It owes its foundations to the writings of the classical masters of equestrianism, especially from the 1700s onward. I took the liberty of illustrating these principles with examples drawing on my own experience in order to demonstrate their practical applications—but, I hope, without distorting their classical origins.

The following pages are meant as a basis for reflection, and a reminder of classical riding theory, to enable you to work with your horse at his best.

To borrow a famous quote from the Buddha[1]: "You yourself must strive. The Buddhas only point the way." It's up to you to pursue your own experience and draw your own conclusions; it's up to you to make the effort to test these principles, see how well they work for you, and perhaps even pass them along to others in your turn.

I could spend pages and pages describing the sensation and the satisfaction of drinking a glass of water on a hot day—but you still wouldn't know what it was like to feel it until you'd experienced it for yourself.

Pirouette, at the walk.

Riding a horse "is a science in its conceptualization and an art in its execution."[2] Here are some elements of that science, taken from what we call "classical" riding, that you can rely on to achieve more, to turn your time on horseback into art. You'll finally be able to experience, preserve, and enrich the long chain of equestrian tradition, as you become a link in that chain yourself.

Ride, and ride again—as often as possible, as many horses as possible, of all types, all conformations. Small, large; young, old; good, less good; schoolmasters, sport horses; in the rain, in the snow, in the searing heat of summer. Surround yourself with teachers, and be curious; watch others, and learn, always, all the time. Each new moment, wherever, whenever, is your next best opportunity to get better. Don't wait—like certain riders who will never make real progress—for the weather to be nice, for a better horse, a better trainer, a better saddle; for the day when you're sleeping better, eating better, more fit. Don't look for excuses not to maximize what you're getting out of your time with your horse—not to maximize your concentration, your effort, and your joy, here and now.

There's always going to be something that isn't perfect, that could be better, that you'd like to (or could) change. So commit to avoiding excuses; it's up to you, in the moment, to be, in the fullest sense of the word. To exist, to listen, to see, to feel, to taste, to smell—to take full advantage of the opportunity offered to you to share your time with a horse. Read these pages on horseback, if you want to, whatever your level. General Alexis François L'Hotte wrote that "riding cannot be learned from books, which only instruct those who already know."[3] There's some truth to those words. That being said, I always prefer to think of the wisdom of Nuno Oliveira: "You have to mount up often, without letting the books get dusty!"[4] Indeed, if riders are learning to ride while on horseback, then they must be learning other things from books: how to reason, how to understand what they're doing, what it is they're looking for from their horses and how to ask for it, and where to look for the answers to future problems, so they can progress beyond what comes "easily" to them.

This book, therefore, is meant to be a guide you can refer to in order to keep the science—the theory, the classical "method" and its principles–fresh in your mind. Read it, reread it, and come back to it as often as you need to until you see what's written between its lines.

Coupled with "the art"—your experiences on horseback, and serious work with competent professionals in the field of training in general and dressage in particular—this book will help you stretch, supple, and relax your horse.

The art of equestrianism begins with perfecting simple things.

Nuno Oliveira

General Considerations

Training and Suppleness

When it comes to the education of the horse, the ultimate goal of training is the same for all riders: to be able to guide the horse in a way that makes the most of his potential. Methods for achieving this goal, on the other hand, differ according to the discipline, sport, or work for which the horse is intended, the rider, the horse.... When forcing the horse to obey is an option within reach of most riders, then quiet, generous acceptance that preserves the character and personality of the horse can only be achieved by a mature and thoughtful rider. There's a fundamental principle every rider should keep in mind: whether in pursuit of suppleness, relaxation, or any other action, the purpose and impact of any given exercise are inseparable from the way in which it's done. Some of the best riders even say that it isn't the exercise that trains, but the way the horse is asked to perform it.

So these stretches and relaxation exercises shouldn't be thought of as an end in themselves. What matters is how they're done, and what they bring to the training of the horse as a result. Some famous French riders didn't use them—Captain Étienne Beudant[5], for example, wrote in his book *Souvenirs Équestres* [Equestrian Memories]: "... [we] recognize that stretching exercises, lateral work in two tracks, etc., are only exercises for the whim and pleasure of the rider. In reality, for ordinary dressage, it's sufficient to teach the horse to

A rare image: the Swiss champion Henri Chammartin, then 65 years old, performing the piaffe.

move forward under the action of the legs and to flex the jaw at the contact of the hand via the reins, because the mouth is 'the fulcrum' that allows the hand to maneuver the levers that produce the gaits and determine the horse's balance.

However, there is no need to work on two tracks to achieve these results: hand to feel the mouth, then leg to create impulsion, then hand, then leg, and so on, until lightness is produced simply by the weight of one rein or the other."

But not everyone is Beudant; exercises geared toward suppleness will be very useful to most riders, provided these exercises are done with an eye to the real objective—to relax. Which exercises you do, and how often you do them, is a choice that will depend on how useful they are to you and your horse, and whether they genuinely improve your horse's way of going. The aim is to encourage ease of handling while helping the horse stay relaxed and light, and the effectiveness of these exercises isn't measured in terms of speed, power, or distance covered...quite the contrary!

To understand how they serve the training of the horse, it's important to be aware of the central "problem" of dressage: the horse is naturally oriented toward his forehand, and his weight is distributed along a horizontal base of support, which predisposes him toward forward motion (running, pulling, and so on).

By her presence alone, the rider helps to overload the forehand even more[6], since around two-thirds of her weight rests there. This balance also favors forward mobility: the mounted horse is even more "on his forehand," and has only one solution—to go faster, straight ahead, in an effort to stay under all this weight. To manage this situation, the rider has to "shape" the horse, physically and psychologically, to allow him to achieve ease in his movements and mobility in all directions at the slightest request of the rider, when mounted.

The training of the horse, therefore, is about making him stronger but also more flexible, so he can lighten his forehand, transfer weight to his hindquarters, and engage and flex his haunches. When his training has progressed far enough, he'll reach a "position of balance [in which he is] ready to move in any direction (as if he were a billiard ball) and equally capable of working with a lengthened or shortened base of support (that is to say, extended gaits are obtained as easily as working gaits or collected gaits)."[7] In other words, the horse will have achieved a kind of balance that allows you to "play any note in the scale" of each gait, from the fullest extension to the loftiest suspension.

This state of balance has a name: it's about **gathering**[8] the horse in a state of **collection**.[9]

To achieve collection, the classical approach in the French tradition rests on three main principles: impulsion, flexibility, and lightness.

"Considered in the abstract," affirms General L'Hotte, "riding is the art of governing the force generated by the muscles of the horse. [...] We will be masters of this force when we know how to combine impulsion with the elastic flexibility of the horse's limbs." However, this flexibility "can only be achieved through training, shaping the muscles, or, if you prefer, the ways in which they move, and bringing their combined actions in tune with each other."[10]

Training a horse, therefore, won't progress far without a solid foundation of gymnastic work, aimed at developing his physical capabilities and his flexibility. Not all horses can achieve a complete ("ideal") degree of collection, but this goal should remain at the heart of your work in the saddle. The exercises that can help you achieve it are suppling, stretching exercises—*relaxation exercises*.

The Reference Point:
The Quality of the Gait

Dressage is the perfecting of the three gaits. The art of equestrianism is the poetry of doing it.

Nuno Oliveira

Gathering the horse into a state of collection, which is the ultimate goal of successful training, can't be done carelessly: if the horse's training isn't carried out according to the principles of classical riding, the horse will never have *a healthy mind in a healthy body*, as the saying goes.

To *gather* the horse doesn't mean *constricting* the horse; and *collection* doesn't mean bringing the horse's head behind the vertical.[11]

In order to achieve extended gaits just as easily as shortened gaits or collected gaits, the horse has to be able to use his physical and mental capabilities to the fullest.

To reach this point, General Albert Decarpentry[12] explains that classical horsemanship progresses through two stages:

– First, it seeks to restore the natural grace of the horse's movements when he's at liberty to the horse under saddle, countering the impact of the weight and the aids of the rider. This stage is focused on targeted gymnastic exercises, with the aim of helping the horse achieve regularity in his gaits and straightness in his bearing.[13] This is traditionally called the **basse**

The word "collection" might seem to imply some compression or constriction; however, when it comes to the carriage of the horse's head, it should be thought of as an "elevation of the neck above the mouth" (1), and not "bringing the head in toward the body" (2).

The pinnacle of the *haut école*: the horse in balance, in a pesade.

école, the "low school," and revolves around improving suppleness and relaxation.

–Second, it endeavors, as Newcastle[14] puts it, to "refine that natural grace into the subtlety of art. This stage guides the horse through progressive lessons in an aesthetic tradition intended to develop the rhythm and harmony of his movements, striving to advance them, little by little, to the point of stylistic perfection—the 'airs of the high school'—while scrupulously respecting their essential character."[15]

Training a horse is a very long process, which must contribute to the "harmonious development of the body and capabilities of the horse."

Relaxation exercises must lead the horse to become calm, supple, and flexible, but also confident, attentive, and perceptive, in aid of achieving a perfect level of understanding with his rider. These qualities can be observed in:

– The straightness and regularity of his gaits.

– The lightness of (the ability to fully support) the forehand and the engagement of the hindquarters, which starts with establishing a degree of impulsion that is always ready to be called upon.

– The willingness of the horse to stay "on the bit," without any tension or resistance—which is to say, in a state of relaxation.

The horse at this level will give the impression that he is "carrying himself," rather than being "carried by his rider." Confident and attentive, he responds with willing generosity to the requests of his rider, remaining absolutely straight in all movements on a straight line, and adjusting his degree of bend to match all curved lines."[16]

You should always keep these goals in mind—they aren't just "nice daydreams" or a piece of abstract classical theory. You'll see them for yourself, as you observe your horse over the course of weeks or months, when the right exercises are incorporated into your horse's training the right way.

The increasing **quality** of your horse's **gaits** under saddle will testify to the quality of your work with your horse. If your horse's gaits are improving over time, you're training him effectively. Conversely, if his gaits get constricted or he starts feeling increasingly stiff, if you feel the need to choose a bit with more leverage or more severe spurs, you should pause and consider what this means: the training strategy you're pursuing may not be right for your horse. You should pause and ask yourself some questions, and consider consulting a professional (or perhaps a different professional, if you're already working with a trainer).

Each of the horse's gaits has its own **biomechanics**, its **qualities** and its **defects**. If your work with your horse is effective, your horse's gaits will match the descriptions in the next section; if your training methods aren't working for your horse, his gaits will "collect" flaws.

Take the walk, for example. If your horse starts losing rhythm more and more in the walk, something's wrong. This is a sign that his back is stiffening up and contracting; you should stop and rethink your approach to training. The walk is a gait with four equal beats—if you walk your horse down the barn aisle with your eyes closed, you should hear four beats (the sound of each hoof hitting the ground) following one another in a regular rhythm, each separated by the same amount of time. Whether your horse is haltered or ridden, on a long rein or with contact, these four beats should always be heard, clearly, distinctly, and at even intervals. The only element that may potentially vary is the length of those four identical intervals; they may all be slightly shorter or slightly longer, depending on whether your horse is at a free walk or being ridden at a specific pace, but all four should still match, either way, and you should always be able to hear them. Otherwise, there's something wrong.

The Walk

The walk is a symmetrical gait that takes place across four equal beats. Its speed is about 3–5 mph (6–8 km/h), or 360 feet per minute (110 meters per minute). The biomechanical sequence of the walk is as follows:

– **First stage:** moving the left hind, with the base of support on the other three feet and focused around the right front.

– **Second stage:** moving the left front, with the base of support on the other three feet and focused around the left hind.

– **Third stage:** moving the right hind, with the base of support on the other three feet and focused around the left front.

– **Fourth stage:** moving the right front, with the base of support on the other three feet and focused around the right hind.

FEI rules[17] define and distinguish between several types of walk: the collected walk, the medium walk, the extended walk, and the free walk.

At the **collected walk**, the horse is "on the bit" and moves forward with intent, with his neck

The correct posture for a horse under saddle

The extended walk, with Henri Chammartin.

rounded and well-supported. His head is on the vertical, and a soft contact is maintained with his mouth. His hindquarters are engaged, with good hock action. The gait of the horse remains a walk, but is energetic, with a regular succession of correct limb positions. Each stride covers less ground than a stride at the medium walk; the collected walk also has higher action, since each joint flexes more and the horse is carrying himself more vigorously. However, while the collected walk may be shorter than the medium walk, so as not to become rushed or irregular, it is also more active.

The **medium walk** is a straight, regular, easy walk with medium extension. The horse "stays on the bit" and walks energetically but calmly, with an even and nimble step, while "tracking up"—with the hind hooves coming to rest in the imprints left by the front hooves.

At the **extended walk**, the horse covers as much ground as possible, without haste and without losing regularity in the rhythm of the walk. The horse should also be overtracking—with the hind hooves landing very clearly in front of the imprints of the front hooves. The rider lets her horse extend his neck and move his head forward without losing an even, steady contact with the mouth.

The **free walk** is a resting gait in which the horse has complete freedom to lower his head and extend his neck (the reins are generally long).

The **quality of the walk** is measured by the distinctness of its four beats, which must be clear, equal, and regular.

The major faults that can be seen at the walk are:
- **The lateral walk**, which is a fault where the horse is moving both feet on one side at the same time or too close to the same time.
- **The jog**, which is a fault of diagonalization where the horse is moving diagonal pairs of feet at the same time or too close to the same time.

The Trot

The trot is a symmetrical gait with a moment of suspension, taking place across two equal beats of diagonal pairs of hooves, separated by that moment of suspension. Its speed varies, but it is typically around 8–9 mph (14–15 km/h) or 650–820 feet per minute (200–250 meters per minute). The biomechanical sequence of the trot is as follows:

- **First stage:** the impact of the left diagonal (the left forefoot and right hind foot).
- **Moment of suspension.**
- **Second stage:** the impact of the right diagonal (the right forefoot and left hind foot).
- **Moment of suspension.**

FEI rules define and distinguish between several types of trot: the collected trot, the working trot, the medium trot, and the extended trot.

At the **collected trot**, the horse is "on the bit" and moves forward with intent, with his neck rounded and well-supported. His clearly engaged hocks maintain the energy of his impulsion, allowing his forehand to move easily in any direction.

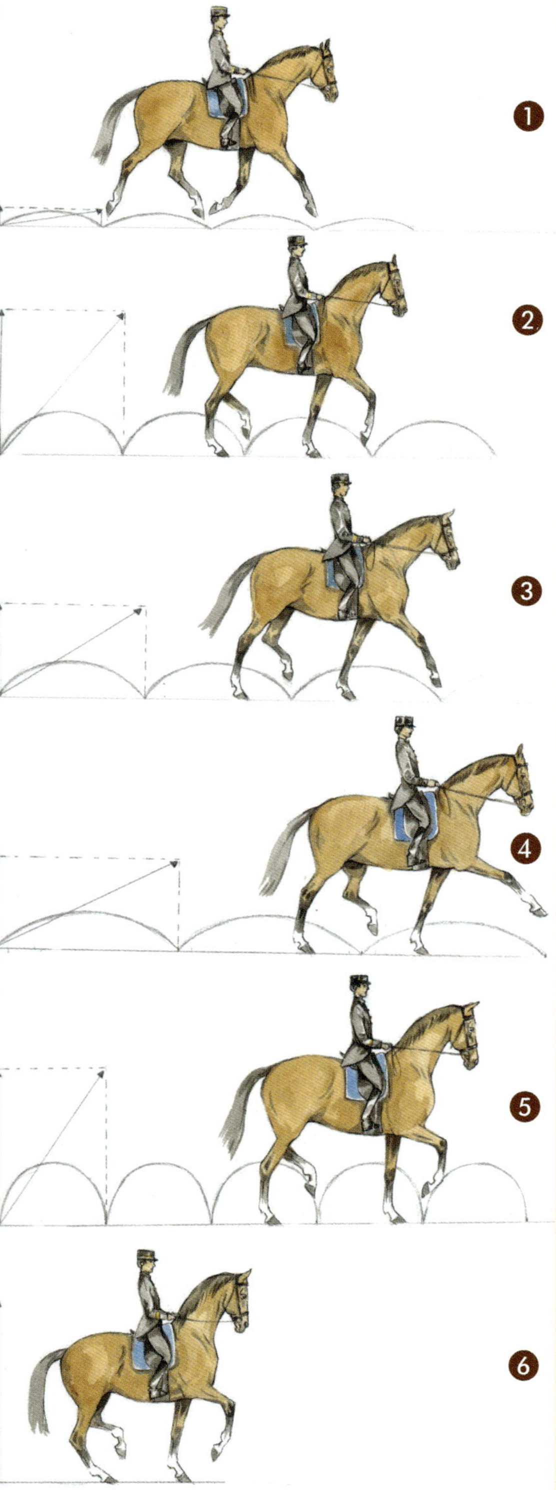

The various trots: **1.** Working trot. **2.** Collected trot. **3.** Medium trot. **4.** Extended trot. **5.** Passage. **6.** Piaffe.

The horse takes shorter strides than in other variations of the trot, but he's lighter and more mobile.

At the **working trot**, the horse carries himself in good balance, remaining "on the bit" and moving forward with equal, elastic strides and active hindquarters—which is to say the importance of impulsion at the working trot, generated by the hindquarters, should be emphasized.

At a **medium trot**, the horse carries himself in a higher, rounder frame than in the working trot. He goes forward readily; his strides are moderately lengthened, and the impulsion coming from the hindquarters is more pronounced. His strides should be as even as possible, and his overall movement should come across as balanced and easy. At a medium trot, the horse should always be overtracking (the hind feet clearly stepping in front of the prints left by the forefeet).

At an **extended trot**, the horse covers the maximum amount of ground. Maintaining the same cadence, he extends his strides to their maximum length, thanks to very strong impulsion from the hindquarters. The rider allows the horse to lower and stretch out his neck, without allowing him to lean on the bit and while remaining in control.

The **quality of the trot** is measured by the overall impression it gives, the regularity and elasticity of the horse's strides—since this depends on the flexibility of the back and the degree of engagement in the hindquarters—and the horse's ability to maintain rhythm and his natural balance, after transitioning from one kind of trot to another. The horse should strike off in the trot, which should always be distinct, active, and regular in its rhythm, without hesitation.

The major faults that can be seen at the trot are:
- The **front "tranter"**: the horse trots with the hind legs but canters with the forelegs.
- The **rear "tranter"**: the horse canters with the hind legs but trots with the forelegs.
- The **disunited trot**: the horse, instead of striking the ground with a diagonal pair of legs simultaneously, strikes with the rear leg and then the foreleg of the diagonal pair, or vice versa.

Circle at canter.

The Canter

The canter is an asymmetrical gait with a moment of suspension, with three unequal beats (the first being the shortest and the third the longest). The horse can canter on the right or left lead. The speed of the canter is typically around 1,150–1,300 feet per minute (350–400 meters per minute), but can range from 980 feet per minute (300 meters per minute) during a show-jumping course to nearly 1,500 feet per minute (450 meters per minute) outside the arena, and up to 2,250 feet per minute (690 meters per minute) on an eventing cross-country course. The biomechanical sequence of the **canter on the right lead** is as follows:

– **First stage:** the impact of the left hind foot.
– **Second stage:** the impact of the left diagonal (the left forefoot and right hind foot).
– **Third stage:** the impact of the right forefoot.
– **Moment of suspension,** during which none of the horse's feet are touching the ground.

The biomechanical sequence of the **canter on the left lead:**
– **First stage:** the impact of the right hind foot.
– **Second stage:** the impact of the right diagonal (the right forefoot and the left hind foot).
– **Third stage:** the impact of the left forefoot.
– **Moment of suspension,** during which none of the horse's feet are touching the ground.

FEI rules define and distinguish between several types of canter: the collected canter, the working canter, the medium canter, and the extended canter.

At a **collected canter**, the horse is "on the bit," with his neck rounded and well-supported. This gait is characterized by lightness in the forehand and engagement of the hindquarters—supple, free, mobile shoulders and very active hips. The horse's strides are shorter than in other types of canter, but the horse is lighter, and his mobility is increased.

The various canters: **1.** Collected canter. **2.** Working canter. **3.** Medium canter. **4.** Extended canter.

At the **working canter**, the horse carries himself in good balance, remaining "on the bit" and moving forward with equal, light, cadenced strides; the hips remain active.

At a **medium canter**, the horse goes forward with vigor; maintaining his balance, he extends his strides, with clear impulsion coming from the hindquarters. His strides should be lengthened, but as regular as possible, with the movement as a whole feeling balanced and easy.

At an **extended canter**, the horse covers the maximum ground. Maintaining the same rhythm, he lengthens his strides as far as possible, without losing his steadiness or his lightness, thanks to powerful impulsion from the hindquarters. The rider, while maintaining a steady contact, allows the horse to lower his head and lengthen his neck; the tip of the horse's nose is more or less forward, without the horse trying to lean on the bit.

The **quality of the canter** is measured by the overall impression it gives, and the regularity and lightness of its triple-time beat—which depend on the horse's acceptance of the bit, his capacity to maintain flexibility in his neck, the engagement of his hindquarters and his active hips, and his ability to maintain rhythm and his natural balance, after transitioning from one kind of canter to another. The horse should also always be completely straight when traveling on straight lines.

The horse should strike off in the canter, which should always be paced and executed with regularity and lightness, without hesitation.

The major faults that can be seen at the canter are:
– The **disunited canter** (cross-cantering): the horse is cantering on the right lead in front but on the left lead in the rear (or vice versa).
– The **no-suspension canter**: there is no moment of suspension between the impacts of the hooves.
– The **four-beat canter**: the horse, instead of striking the ground with a diagonal pair of legs simultaneously, strikes with the rear leg and then the foreleg of the diagonal pair, or vice versa.

Important Recommendations

Never use force. [...] The secret, in riding, is to act little, and always to a purpose. The more we do, the worse it gets. The less we do, the better.

Nuno Oliveira

1. Relaxation exercises are used to soften[18]—to relax and lengthen the muscles to develop their elasticity, because a muscle is contracted more easily when it is long and relaxed first. The reverse isn't true: a muscle that's compressed and contracted for too long loses its elasticity and gets harder to stretch. The important thing isn't for your horse to perform any given exercise precisely as it's described in the "manual," but for him to develop flexibility, suppleness, and ease of movement: this result should be your guide. You should certainly aim for a "textbook" execution, but you should never force your horse. As he becomes more flexible, with time, he'll be able to give you something closer and closer to the ideal.

2. Any exercise that requires an effort, or requires a position that tests an area of habitual stiffness or a conformational limitation, always causes—and very quickly—discomfort, then fatigue, and then suffering, in the parts of the body that are directly affected or are compensating for the horse's difficulties. These kinds of exercises shouldn't be asked of the horse for very long; carefully balance the degree of effort you're requesting, and offer release at the smallest result, to avoid strain and fatigue.

3. Forcing the horse into a constrained position for a long time always causes, in the end, loss of impulsion, tightness in the muscles, and compensatory issues. It's frequent repetition of the same exercise, performed under good conditions and alternated with periods of complete relaxation on a long rein, that creates progress. So all movements should be followed by a period of rest, at a free walk, with the reins left long.

4. "Any movement badly performed is not only useless, but harmful."[19] In order for relaxation exercises to be useful, three conditions must be met: there must be impulsion (without haste), unconditional respect for the gait, and relaxation. Any softening carried out with a loss of impulsion, in haste, or under physical constraint, destroys harmony of movement and makes future progress more difficult.

5. Before starting an exercise, you must have a clear idea of what you're trying to achieve, the means (positions and timing of your aids) you need to achieve it, and the problems you're likely to encounter in the attempt. Whatever movement you're requesting, its proper execution by the horse depends on your aids—on the ways your hands and legs direct and harmonize the horse's motion—and on the appropriateness of your choices of which aid to use when, at what intensity.

6. Every horse is an individual; you'll have to make a choice when it comes to the range of the stretches you want to attempt in your relaxation exercises. Any given degree of stretch or effort can be excellent for one horse and catastrophic for another. You have to keep in mind the objective of each exercise, the movements it requires, and whether you need to adapt either one (the exercise or its methods) to your horse.

7. Generally speaking, when a joint is flexed, it's not the muscles that flex it that are being relaxed, but the muscles that *oppose* its flexion, since they're the muscles being stretched. So if you want to correct a stiffness on the left, you need to bend your horse to the right; you're not softening the right side, but rather lengthening the muscles on the left, by stretching them.

8. Remember, "flexibility is, above all, a function of elasticity in the [horse's] back, which contributes even at the walk. The back is elastic when it has been trained in such a way that the energy of the hindquarters is transmitted harmoniously through the croup, loins, back,

Always work with confidence and calm.

withers, and nuchal ligament to reach the neck, and end at the rider's hand.

When the back doesn't make this contribution to the walk, the horse propels himself only by the motion of his limbs, animated in a pendular way [by his weight]. It follows that his gaits are stiff."[20]

9. You have to carefully assess the amount you can ask of the horse each day—starting from the baseline of the previous day. Just ask for that much again, and see how it goes today.

10. Don't hesitate to ask for less, either, if you run into difficulty (on a new movement, or a familiar one). Don't fixate on meeting the standard given in an exercise if it's causing problems. It's better to back up to an earlier stage where your horse can move in a state of relaxation than to try to force progress in a way that creates strain or constriction.

11. Always start simple, and progress to the more difficult. Keep the horse's gait regular and relaxed, set your expectations for the horse's self-carriage in line with the level you've reached (collection, partial collection, on the bit, mostly on the bit), and maintain it on a straight line. Then make sure it's maintained during transitions from walk to trot, or canter, and vice versa. If all this goes well, you can tackle more complex maneuvers, always starting with the simplest ones—while keeping in mind that any change in the horse's way of going during work could be a sign of discomfort. In this case, before going any further, immediately try to understand the origin of the discomfort; don't continue with the movement. Ease off, and allow the horse to relax until the discomfort disappears. Then try again, with the correct carriage and way of going restored, and see whether you can complete the movement this time.[21]

12. Prioritize slowness. Slow movements become greater than the sum of their parts. Between a slightly too-fast gait and a slightly too-slow gait, you should always choose the slow gait (provided there isn't a decrease in energy, only in speed) in order to create true relaxation. When he is moving slowly, the horse can take the time to understand, to move deliberately, and to become flexible; none of this is possible at a fast pace.

13. Finally, "the use of suppling exercises must be undertaken with the conformation of the horse in mind."[22]

"Whatever the skill of the rider, no exercise can replace the work of time. Patience and a gradual increase in effort create a considerable benefit in dressage: going slowly *is* going fast."[23]

"Many times, it is the rider who prevents the horse from executing a certain exercise correctly, by using the aids incorrectly and by taking up the wrong position[24]."

14. Relaxation exercises for horses require as much gentleness as you would use when stretching your own body. To experience this for yourself, stand on a level surface with your feet approximately shoulder-width apart, and, leaning forward, try to touch your toes with your fingers, without bending your legs. If you can do this easily, then go further, and try putting your palms flat on the floor. However flexible you may be, you'll be aware that you need to move slowly and patiently, without rushing your spine, joints, muscles, or tendons—you'll want to stop when you feel the "pull" at the backs of your knees and thighs. To improve your flexibility, you have to stretch these muscles a little bit; so try to go slightly farther, but with even more softness and care, even more slowly. Otherwise, it would be painful—which would be a sign that you've damaged some of your tissues or joints. It's the same for the horse.

15. Suppling, stretching exercises for the horse should always be carried out **calmly**, **slowly**, **gently**, and in a state of **relaxation**. "When sweat appears," wrote Captain de Saint-Phalle,[25] "that means the man has overshot the mark!" Proceed with patience and never underestimate the effort your horse is putting into his work. After each exercise, allow the horse to walk on a long rein for the same amount of time the exercise took; this is a good safeguard against overwork.

Types of Relaxation Exercises

Dressage isn't about performing difficult movements, but rather making the horse more receptive and more flexible, and giving him the ability to carry himself in balance.

Nuno Oliveira

There are many, many relaxation exercises out there, if only because basic stretching and suppling movements can be infinitely combined and recombined with each other. It's worth mentioning the distinction between *localized* stretching and relaxation, and *full-body* stretching and relaxation.

Localized stretching addresses only one part of the horse's body. The set of flexion exercises developed by that respected classical equestrian of the nineteenth century, François Baucher,[26] belongs in this category. This book doesn't deal with these localized exercises; while they can be effective in the hands of experts, they can also be harmful to the horse if done incorrectly. If you want to use exercises like these, you need to consult a rider or trainer who specializes in classical equestrian technique and can show you in person how to execute them, taking the necessary precautions.

Full-body stretching is aimed at the whole horse, involving the entire musculoskeletal system. These stretches are done in motion, with a calm, relaxed horse who's in front of the leg, on the aids and on the bit.[27] Relaxation exercises in this category are the focus of this book.

These exercises can also be divided, theoretically, into two categories:

– **"Longitudinal" relaxation exercises**, which mobilize the horse along the length of his body.

– **Lateral relaxation exercises**, which mobilize the sides of the horse's body.

The principal stages of raising the forehand and collecting the horse. **1.** Young horse. **2.** Early collection. **3.** Increased flexion of the hips. **4.** Piaffe. **5.** Levade.

Karen Tébar and Fallada performing a half-pass in trot, to the left.

The Purpose of Longitudinal Relaxation Exercises

These exercises improve the flexibility of the vertebral column—and, as a result, increase the engagement of the hindquarters and the mobility of the hips—by enhancing the range of motion of the sacroiliac and coxo-femoral joints. These joints are what allows (or doesn't allow) the horse to bring his hocks underneath his body to support his weight, and they give the horse control over how much ground he covers, through an increase or decrease in the energy transferred from his hindquarters. Beyond serving as the source of impulsion, the hips become "a genuine rudder that presides over changes in direction."[28]

The hindquarters are able to move laterally, and not through a passive "skidding" by the croup, but via the engagement of the haunches, and the lowering of the hip and flexion of the hock on one side.

The range of longitudinal relaxation exercises includes all transitions from one gait to another, or within the same gait (lengthening or collecting), from the simplest to the most complex; halting; backing; extending the neck; lowering the neck; counter-canter; and working on a slope (whether you're going uphill or down).

The Purpose of Lateral Relaxation Exercises

These exercises relax and soften the horse's sides and help the horse's muscles work symmetrically; they also give the rider a greater ability to direct the haunches, and, as a result, straighten the horse. The basis for lateral stretches is working the horse on a circle; they should be tackled only once the horse maintains elastic contact with the rider's hand at all times (when he is consistently "on the bit"[29]), and when he understands the meaning of aids given with one leg only. These exercises will let the rider confirm whether the horse is round, and assess his position and the way in which he's holding his back.

The range of lateral relaxation exercises includes, above all, voltes and work on a circle (15 meters maximum) and on curving lines, and all the exercises that are derived from those basics: larger or smaller circles, riding corners, serpentines, changes of direction, widening circles, and lateral movements of the hips or shoulders on a circle—which serve as the basis for the turn-on-the-forehand[30] and turn-on-the-haunches.[31]

Finally, the category of lateral relaxation exercises also includes the standard two-track lateral movements. In order of difficulty:

– **Leg-yield.**
– **Shoulder-in** and related exercises: shoulder-fore, shoulder-in on three tracks, shoulder-in on four

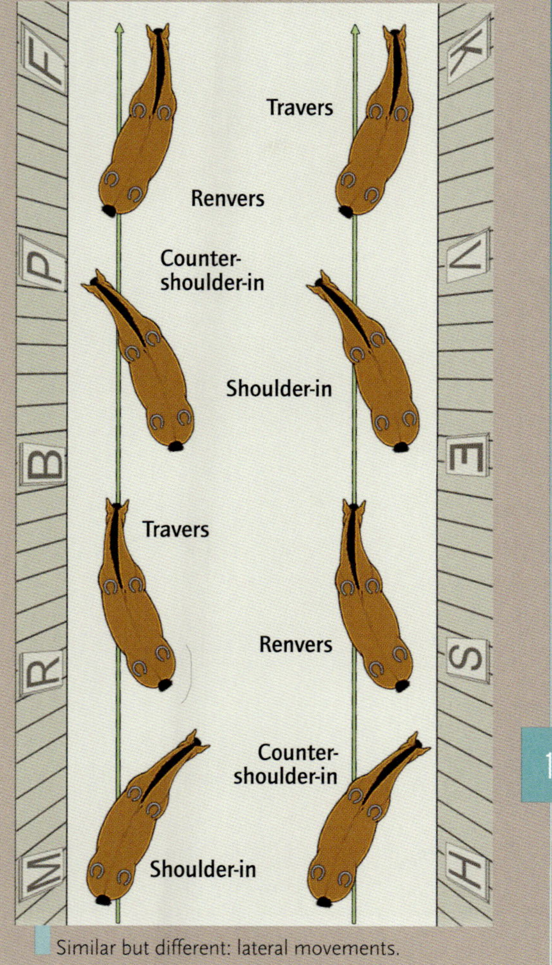

Similar but different: lateral movements.

tracks, counter-shoulder-fore, counter-shoulder-in on three tracks, counter-shoulder-in on four tracks.
– **Half-pass** and related exercises: haunches-in (travers) and haunches-out (renvers).

The Benefits of Work on Two Tracks

– It refines the horse's responsiveness to the aids.
– It makes the horse more flexible as a whole, by increasing the freedom of the shoulders, the suppleness of the hindquarters, and the elasticity of the connection that runs from the mouth to the neck, down the neckline and along the back, to the hips.
– It improves rhythm and cadence.
– It harmonizes the horse's balance and gait.
– It develops and increases the engagement of the hindquarters.

One can, by poking and prodding and pulling, obtain a stretch. But to be useful, stretching must not be forced—otherwise, we lose all the benefits of any preceding work.

Nuno Oliveira

Longitudinal Relaxation Exercises

Transitions

Definitions

A *transition* is a shift from one gait to another, or a change of amplitude in the same gait (which is referred to as "a transition within the gait"). Transitions encourage responsiveness and mobility in the horse.

They should be clear, smooth, and without abruptness; you have to keep an eye on the position of the neck (its stability—or instability—will let you know whether the transition poses a problem for your horse) and maintain the rhythm of the gait appropriately (the cadence of the previous gait should remain intact until the instant the horse takes up the new gait or comes to a halt). Also, take care to ask for downward transitions with the chest more than with the hands.

The degree of difficulty here depends on the transition you're trying to achieve, and on your horse's level of training.

Generally speaking, practicing transitions is just as important for the horse and for the rider:
— They encourage the horse to pay attention to the aids of the legs and hands.
— They make it possible to soften the back (and a flexible back allows transitions without head tilting or shaking, with greater stability in the forehand).
— They invite greater involvement from the hindquarters, during transitions to a slower gait.
— They promote relaxation in the hocks, and, in general, greater activity in the hips, during lengthening.

– For the rider, they're a driving lesson: "they teach [the rider] to create, maintain, and regulate impulsion, and to give aids that act or release independently from each other."[32]

No matter what transition you're riding, up or down, you have to achieve stability in the forehand. You won't get it by clenching your fingers tight around your reins; it's a combination of all kinds of important elements, including the way the horse is holding his back, the flexibility of the back, the degree of activity in the hips, and much more. The most important contribution, though, comes from the momentum "contained" in the gait before the transition happens. If the horse goes from walk to trot while raising his head, there wasn't enough impulsion in the walk. Conversely, when you go from trot to walk, you have to keep the momentum of the trot, and release as soon as the transition comes while maintaining the contact.

For young horses, as for young riders, transitions must be approached with this principle in mind: hand without leg, leg without hand. It's only logical, when working with a young horse, to avoid using the "brake" at the same time as the "accelerator," and for the rider, it's worthwhile to practice keeping the aids independent, and to experience their effects one at a time. "By avoiding the simultaneous use of the hand and the legs, [the rider can ensure] the horse understands more clearly what is asked of him, and the rider is obliged to be more precise in the use of her aids, because any errors she commits are immediately apparent to her without delay."[33]

In all cases, "the position comes before the action," and you should always indicate your intentions to your horse by positioning yourself to apply the aids (sitting up tall to slow down, shifting your body weight, arranging your legs to signal canter, and so on) before you actually apply them.

Transitions from One Gait to Another

Transitions from one gait to another are assessed according to their difficulty. In general, they're approached in order following this progression:

– First, halt/walk/halt, walk/trot/walk, trot/canter/trot.
– Then halt/trot, trot/halt, canter/walk.
– Then backing up/walk, backing up/trot.
– Finally canter/walk, canter/halt, halt/canter, backing up/canter.

This classification, is very loose, because the actual difficulty of any given transition, in practice, depends on the "level" of the gait and the degree of precision requested by the rider. So the transition from working trot to halt may be easier than the transition from working trot to collected trot; by contrast, if the transition from working trot to collected trot is "easy" for an experienced horse, that doesn't mean it isn't going to be very complicated for a youngster learning it for the first time. And you won't require the same things from a canter-to-trot transition for a young horse who's just begun training as you will from the same transition with an older horse.

How to Perform a Downward Transition

Sit up tall, raising yourself upward, and, while decreasing the motion of your pelvis, use your "hands"[34] to gently discourage forward motion. Your horse will slow down and transition to the lower gait. The voice can be a valuable help in reducing the amount of action needed from the hands. The legs should remain in contact with the horse's body, without pressing or closing, because:
– It isn't logical, from the perspective of the young horse.
– You should try to keep your aids as simple as possible.
– You should always aim to reduce the intensity necessary in repeated requests for the same result.
– A well-prepared transition (adapted to the appropriate level of dressage) rarely requires a significant use of aids.
– This is how you will achieve lightness.
– If the horse makes his transitions without engagement, or stumbles in transition, you can, request the same transitions in shoulder-fore.

– Your horse's transitions will become clean with work and time.

How to Perform an Upward Transition

An upward transition is requested through the action of the legs[35] (and potentially a vocal cue). Maintain the contact with the horse's mouth, without moving your hands either forward or backward. Be careful not to keep your fingers closed on the reins, which would force the horse to strike off from a halt into a trot, or from a walk to a canter, against the hand.

Once the simpler transitions feel easy to you, you can perform them closer together, which will increase your horse's responsiveness and attentiveness. After that, you can also try more complex transitions (halt/trot or walk/canter, for example) as your dressage training progresses, mastering the upward transitions before their downward equivalents.

Lengthening at trot.

23

Mistakes During Downward Transitions	Mistakes During Upward Transitions
Mistakes by the Rider	**Mistakes by the Rider**
– Leaning back (which strains the horse's back and leads to disengagement of the horse's hindquarters and loss of roundness). – Leaning forward (this often causes the rider's legs to move backward). – Pulling on the reins (this contracts the horse's forehand, which also leads to tension and a loss of roundness). – Not preparing properly for the transition (this means the horse won't be ready for it, and the transition will be either hesitant or rushed as a result).	– Leaning forward, fidgeting. – Pulling on the reins and giving aids with your legs at the same time. – Trying to maintain the horse's head carriage by closing your fingers on the reins. – Not preparing properly for the transition.
Mistakes by the Horse	**Mistakes by the Horse**
– Crossing his legs during the transition (performing it in shoulder-fore). – Making hesitant transitions. – Not striking off with energy in the new gait (the action of the legs needs to be addressed, if this is due to a lack of impulsion; it's a matter of patience, if the horse is young; and the aids may need to be refined, if this is due to muddled cues from the rider).	– Lacking clarity or rhythm in the new gait (review and refine the aids, ensure he has enough impulsion). – Inconsistency in the contact and movement of the head (review and refine the aids, work on roundness and relaxation).

Arnaud Serre et Hélio II transitioning from collected canter to pirouette.

Transitions within a Gait

The term "transition within a gait" refers to changes in the degree of extension or collection while riding the same gait.

Whatever the gait, "extension" doesn't mean "rushing." In an extended gait, the horse increases the lengths of his strides (which therefore cover more ground than before) while maintaining a cadence[36] identical to the cadence of the working gait. Rushing, by contrast, means the horse is just going faster—not lengthening his strides, only taking more of them and doing it more quickly, which means his cadence is going to accelerate. When a horse rushes this way, his withers collapse, his back turns hollow, and his hindquarters disengage.

The difference will be obvious to most riders who have a little experience; but if you aren't sure, you can count the number of strides your horse needs to cross the diagonal of the arena (for example) in his working gait, and then ride it again and count his strides in his extended gait. If the second number is smaller, then that means your horse's stride length increased—since he needed fewer strides to cover the same amount of ground—and you're headed in the right direction.

Generally speaking, you should be happy with the best your horse can give you. If you try to force him to give you more, you'll only cause distress, discomfort, or both, which will always lead to tension and a duller, less responsive attitude. Ask for extension "by lowering the belt [of the rider's pants] forward, without putting the shoulders too far back."[37]

Don't push while the horse is in extension, or you'll lose momentum. You have to "store" impulsion in advance, during the preparation along the short side of the arena and in the corner preceding the transition to the extended gait.

The self-carriage of the horse changes, in extension, because it's dependent on the length of his stride. In collected gaits, *the neck rises*, allowing greater engagement of the hindquarters. In extended gaits, *the neck stretches out*, allowing the horse full use of the muscles of his topline, which lets him lengthen with ease.

An extended walk is correct when the horse changes:
– His frame: he must stretch out, lengthen his neck, and move the tip of his nose forward and down.
– His stride length: his strides have to get longer without the cadence of his gait changing. In addition to the counting method described above, you can check the length of your horse's stride by looking at his hoofprints; in the extended walk, as in the extended trot, he should be overtracking.

How to Perform an Extended Walk

It's important to maintain your upright position in order to avoid weighting the horse's forehand (in which case he'll start rushing instead of extending). Use your leg aids and your seat, increasing the motion of your pelvis,[38] and gradually open your fingers around the reins, allowing the tip of the horse's nose to reach forward and letting the horse stretch out his neck. As mentioned, it's essential for the horse to be able to extend his neck—apart from the fact that this is a judging criterion for the extended walk, it's also what allows the horse to lengthen his stride fully and achieve the extension you're asking him for. When the horse begins to extend, help him lengthen even further by relaxing your abdomen completely, so you're following his

motion—and only following, without pushing and jostling him out of his rhythm.

To slow down, reduce the following motion of your pelvis and abdomen, straighten your upper body, and gradually shorten your reins, asking for the transition "with the chest and not the hands."[39]

> **In extension, your horse should be overtracking.**
> *As a reminder:*
> – Your horse is **tracking up** when his hind hoof lands in the hoofprint of the front hoof on the same side.
> – Your horse is **undertracking** when his hind hoof lands short of the hoofprint of the front hoof on the same side.
> – Your horse is **overtracking** when his hind hoof lands ahead of the hoofprint of the front hoof on the same side.

The lengthening of the horse's neck and the increase in his stride length, when you open your fingers on your reins, are two important indicators of a good extension at the walk—and they also confirm that your training is on the right track, if your horse willingly extends into the space your opened fingers give him.

Mistakes in the Extended Walk

Mistakes by the Rider

– Suddenly letting go of the reins (and losing the contact).
– Letting the horse lose his impulsion.
– Moving too much, fidgeting.
– Failing to give the horse space to move into, and failing to move with him (which will disrupt his balance, and also create problems when it's time to "gather" the horse back in at the end of the extended walk).
– Asking for the extended walk too timidly.

Mistakes by the Horse[40]

– Rushing, or transitioning all the way to trot.
– Losing the contact.
– Making errors in gait sequence.
– Losing engagement.
– Losing rythm and regularity, or drifting laterally.
– Positioning the head at the vertical or behind the vertical.

Working trot: the rider prepares to practice the gait.

How to Perform an Extended Trot

You need to let your horse bring his head forward and lengthen his neck a little bit—but don't let him go all the way into a full extension of his neckline. The extension[41] of a gait "is a forward and downward contact, but it is not about letting go of the reins. [...] In extension, the horse must lengthen his neck a little but remain rounded[42] and in your hand. Extension at the trot (when done on the diagonal) benefits from being preceded by shoulder-in or haunches-out (in the corner or along one side of the arena); these movements "compress" your horse, so to speak, which means all you need to do is open your fingers and allow your horse to "release" that impulsion and use that energy to lengthen himself on the diagonal. If he starts at a canter or gets "carried away" by his own speed and energy, then above all, you must avoid punishing him by bringing him firmly to a halt, because this will discourage him from developing as much impulsion in the future.

Instead, put him into shoulder-in, which will lead him to slow down on his own as he engages his hindquarters, or guide him into a circle and

Ideally, extension only occurs when the horse is able to remain rhythmic in his working trot, and stays round, with a flexible back that rises, instead of tightening. The first requests for extension should be made only at the rising trot.

then make that circle smaller and smaller until, again, he naturally slows down on his own. Then resume at the trot, and ask for the extended trot again, more gradually, with less intensity.

The extended trot is at its most valuable if your horse is increasing the length of his moment of suspension with very strong thrust from the hindquarters, and good horizontal balance. The result will be the natural extension of the forelegs forward, because they are "looking for the ground."

To drop out of the extended trot, ask in the same way as at the walk, straightening your torso and shortening the reins. The voice can be a useful aid,[43] and can replace, through repetition, the action of your hands—limiting the amount of direct action by the rider on the body of the horse.

Mistakes in the Extended Trot

Mistakes by the Rider

– Suddenly letting go of the reins (and losing the contact).
– Letting the horse lose his impulsion.
– Moving too much, fidgeting.
– Failing to give the horse space to move into, and failing to move with him (which will disrupt his balance, and also create problems when it's time to "gather" the horse back in at the end of the extended trot).
– Asking for the extended trot too timidly.
– Letting the neck stretch out too far (so much so that the horse becomes unbalanced).

Mistakes by the Horse

– Losing rhythm and regularity, or moving with asymmetry.
– Failing to respond, failing to change his way of going.
– Moving jerkily, with the motions of the forelegs starting from the knees instead of from the shoulders (this is an indication that the horse is hollow, and therefore lacking roundness).

How to Perform an Extended Canter

The principles of extension at the canter are the same as at the trot, but—as at the walk—you need to be careful to follow the horse's movement smoothly. The real difficulty of extension at the canter (apart from problems caused by asking for it too timidly) comes less from the extension itself and more from gathering the horse again at the end of the extended canter to slow him down: it's almost always the hardest thing, slowing down.

All too often, we develop the canter without worrying about straightness. However, when we ask him to extend, the horse will tend to shift laterally (which is to say he'll move his hips toward the inside of the track, adopting a position that feels natural to him), which makes it impossible to gather him back up properly at the end of the extended canter.[44] To avoid this, when asking for extension and when bringing extension to an end, the horse should be kept in shoulder-fore.

In any case, **be satisfied with your horse's best effort to give you what you're asking for**. If you don't think he's extending his gait enough, or if his extension doesn't meet your expectations, be careful not to press him for more than he's able to offer—this could disrupt his rhythm, throw off his balance, or teach him to develop his gait with his back tense and hollow, which will inevitably reduce his ability to engage and any possibility of improving his extended gaits going forward. It's better by far to return to the working gait, prepare, and try again. If you take care to relax the horse, this "accordion" sequence (lengthening for a few strides, returning to the working gait, and then lengthening again) will naturally and gradually develop your horse's ability to extend well.

Keep in mind that it's always best not to "extend" more than you can "regather" at the end of the extended gait. If slowing down is posing a problem, don't force it with your hands—guide the horse into a movement that will slow him naturally, such as shoulder-in. Here, again, the "accordion" sequence can help you: practice both going into and collecting the horse out of extension, without pushing to the point where slowing down is difficult, and you'll improve your horse's ability to manage extension, a bit at a time.

Finally, you can also:
– Alternate lengthening the horse and collecting him again at gradually decreasing intervals, to help bring the horse's hindquarters under him during the latter and relax his haunches and hocks during the former.
– Ask for clearer and more distinct lengthening and collection, to develop your horse's strength and to get a feel for how to "balance" the horse between your hands and your legs.

> "A horse that speeds up or slows down by raising his neck is performing anything but equitation."
> "To perform passage, all the books say the horse must keep his neck at the same height, but I want more: I want the horse to make this transition while keeping the same state of mind."
>
> Nuno Oliveira

This horse is moving in the extended canter and preparing to drop back down into the working canter.

– Repeat these exercises on the circle,[45] once they come easily when ridden on straight lines.

The Halt

The rider low in the saddle, with the reins at the appropriate length and the elbows close to the body, will stop her horse by pushing with the seat and the back, and bringing the belt buckle forward.

Nuno Oliveira

At the halt, your horse should be motionless and square on all four legs, with his neck arched without stiffness, the poll high, and the head a little bit in front of the vertical. He maintains a soft contact with the rider's hand, quietly chews his bit, and is ready to move forward at the slightest indication but remains at the halt if you salute or let go of your reins.

The difficulty of attaining a halt varies, depending on the gait you're in when you ask for it.

Generally speaking, practicing the halt develops calmness and responsiveness to the aids.

The halt should be achieved "by the displacement of the horse's weight to the hindquarters by a properly increased action of the seat and legs of the athlete, driving the horse toward a softly closed hand, causing an almost instantaneous but not abrupt halt at a previously fixed place." This definition, from Article 402 of the FEI rules, describes an ideal that only applies to high-level competition horses and riders. Reading it yourself, you might get the impression that in order to halt correctly, you have to slow the horse with your hands while also pushing him along with your legs, so he's engaged even at the halt. However, that's not quite accurate, because applying this principle in its letter, rather than its spirit, can cause several problems:
– The young horse is unlikely to understand what the rider wants to achieve by applying the "brakes" and the "accelerator"[46] at the same time.
– There's a risk of teaching the horse to "listen" to the aid that acts the most—so it will then take more action with the hands than the legs to

Halt square and straight.

achieve a halt, but more action with the legs than the hands to keep the horse engaged ...
– There's also a risk that the horse will evade the hand or lose engagement in the legs; sometimes, he'll commit himself to stopping so much that he starts to pose like a mountain goat on a cliffside, a bearing that's hard to keep up and won't make it easy for him to strike off again. He may end up adopting all sorts of odd ways of going—refusing to engage at all (not responding to the leg aids), for example, or "parking" the hindquarters with an extra step as soon as he's brought to a halt.

As with transitions, it's better not to use your hands at the same time as your legs. When asking for a halt, the legs should remain in contact with the horse, but without tightening or loosening. The rider should only actively "close" with the legs in unusual circumstances—when your horse has disengaged in the hind end, for example, you may want to halt in shoulder-fore, which will keep the hindquarters reaching underneath the horse.[47]

The essential thing is to take your time. The halt must be practiced very gently at first. Be undemanding with horses who have their necks "inverted," who are nervous or shifting their weight, and in general with all horses who don't have sufficient musculature yet to achieve the perfect halt.

How to Perform a Walk/Halt Transition

Sit up straight (as for any transition), and push with your seat and your back while bringing what would be your belt buckle forward and down. This will allow your arms to follow the motion of your torso fully. At the same time, you'll be able to use your reins independently to request a halt. Release the aids as soon as you feel the transition beginning. Since the walk is a four-beat gait, you need to allow time for all four feet to complete the last stride. On a hard surface (a paved road, for example), you should be able to hear four final beats as you halt, corresponding to each hoof positioning itself for the halt.

How to Perform a Trot/Halt Transition

During the trot/halt transition, the most common mistake riders make is bracing themselves backward and pulling on the reins in an effort to make sure the horse comes to a complete stop. This only serves to put pressure on your horse's back, which limits the engagement of the hindquarters and creates extra torque on the forehand, causing the withers to sink and destroying any roundness in the horse's self-carriage. It also increases the odds that your horse will resist the halt, weight his forehand, and disengage his hindquarters. To succeed at a trot/halt transition, you have to approach it the same way as a walk/halt transition,

The essentials for a good halt:
– Prepare for the halt by collecting the gait to slow the horse down; think of it as if you're converting the length of the horse's strides (forward) into elevation (up and down) until the length of his strides is zero.

Halt square and straight.

Once your horse is able to halt calmly and smoothly, you can work on making him rounder. For this to be effective, he must already be able to achieve roundness and some degree of lightness in the shoulder-in, renvers, travers, and half-pass.[48] Start by asking for the halt in shoulder-in and in travers, in order to teach him to "tuck" his hindquarters under himself. Then ask for the halt during the half-pass, following this sequence: ride down the centerline, half-pass to the track, halt.

Backing Up

When the horse halts squarely, with his haunches engaged, in a state of lightness, he will strike off the same way into the walk or the trot, without altering the position of his head and neck; this is the moment to start asking him to back up.

Nuno Oliveira

Backing up is a symmetrical movement, in which the horse's legs pick up and move in diagonal pairs, with the horse remaining straight and keeping his hips slightly lowered. If done correctly—in lightness—it enhances the relaxation and suppleness of the back and loins achieved by the other transitions, and allows you to shift your horse's balance to his haunches while encouraging his responsiveness to the aids.

The quality of this movement is determined by the quality of the halt that precedes it. If the horse didn't halt squarely, or the hindquarters are too engaged or disengaged in the halt, backing up isn't likely to go well.

The first steps in backing up are generally done in-hand; once the horse backs up easily, while remaining calm, straight, relaxed, and light, then you should attempt to ask him to back up under saddle.[49]

To ask the horse to back up while you're riding him, you need to start from a light, square stop. Close your legs, and, a fraction of a second later, engage "the action of the torso, the waist, and the reins"[50]; as soon as the horse begins to back up, reward him with a pat and let him move forward again, with the reins long.

with a clear understanding of the correct position for your horse at the halt. The idea is to maintain the energy of the gait right up until the moment of the halt, as if you wanted to go into the piaffe. Your horse will then halt with engagement. It can only be done correctly with horses trained to a level that allows them to be ridden straight and collected in the canter. The canter should then be slowed, using shoulder-in, until the gait has been brought "down to earth" and the halt feels natural.

Mistakes in the Halt
Mistakes by the Rider
– Pulling on the reins to bring the horse to a halt by "dragging" him to a stop (instead of maintaining the horse's energy). – Leaning backward (and thereby overloading the horse's back) instead of sitting up tall. – Rushing the halt. – Failing to prepare enough for the transition to the halt.
Mistakes by the Horse
– Failing to halt squarely (this may mean you need to work on the coordination of the aids, or that you need to increase the horse's responsiveness by progressing to the halt more gradually, or even try halting in shoulder-fore to encourage engagement of the horse's hindquarters on the side to which his croup is moving). – Failing to commit fully to the halt (in which case you should practice halts in shoulder-fore).

30

Backing up on a horse that's staying round and on the bit (1), and on a horse that's hollow (2).

The legs don't need to do anything else; they should remain "closed," monitoring the direction in which the horse is backing and forming a "corridor" through which the horse is moving. The horse should stop backing up as soon as you resume sitting normally and open your fingers around your reins. When backing up, avoid leaning backward, pulling on the horse's mouth, or making him raise his head, as any of these will overload the horse's hindquarters.

Rather, it should be "with a relaxed horse, starting to back up, beginning by alternately using one rein and then both reins, being satisfied at first with a step or two, rewarding [the horse], and then starting again."[51] If you're working with a young horse, or a weak or tense horse, you can lean forward slightly and let him lower his head, to help encourage him to round his back and hindquarters.

In some schools of equestrian thought, riders are taught to keep their hands in a fixed position and resist lowering them, by repeatedly closing their fingers on their reins as the horse's foreleg on the same side rises (visible at the shoulder). This principle is valid, but only for very experienced riders, as long as the hands are soft and the horse is perfectly straight.

In general, you shouldn't attempt to back your horse until he's moving easily and without hesitation when you ask him for forward movements. The horse also needs to be constantly ready to resume forward movement, without pauses, stiffness, or abruptness, at your request.

Given the dangers of backing up (in particular, the risk of settling too much weight in the

Mistakes When Backing

Mistakes by the Rider

– Pulling on the reins to force the horse backward (this will probably only lead the horse to refuse more emphatically, or to weight his hindquarters too deeply so that he's practically sitting).
– Maintaining the halt too long before backing, which deprives the horse of momentum.
– Being too hard in the leg when it's time to ask the horse to go forward again (this may take the horse by surprise and result in him "freezing" instead of striking off).

Mistakes by the Horse

"Any anticipation or haste in the movement, any resistance or defensive response to the hand, any deviation of the hips, any widening or laziness of the hindquarters, and any 'dragging' of the forelegs are serious faults."[54]

hindquarters), it shouldn't be done for dozens of yards at a time,[52] as you may sometimes see. Once the horse is able to respond appropriately to your request to back up, it would be better to focus your efforts on "swinging the horse between backward and forward, at the walk, by taking only a few steps of each of them."[53] This will allow you to encourage balance, impulsion, lightness, and, later on, the "diagonalization" that will lead to piaffe. With a hot horse, it's absolutely necessary to follow any backward movement by moving forward, and then allowing the horse a rest period at the walk, with the reins long.

Working "Long and Low"

This work, which is recommended for horses with too-high necks and hollow backs above all, is good for all young horses.

Nuno Oliveira

Working "long and low," with the neckline lowered and extended, is classified among the longitudinal relaxation exercises. Your horse is "long and low" when, having relaxed in his jaw, he gradually lengthens his neck and extends his head to seek the contact with the bit that he's used to; then, without picking up or slowing his gait, he lowers the tip of his nose forward and downward, to approximately the height of his knees. The goal of this exercise is to get the horse used to extending his neck when he wants to cover ground, and rounding it to slow down, halt, or enhance specific movements. This work is only really useful if you alternate it with asking the horse to raise and round his neck and lower his center of gravity.

Asking the horse to lower his neck is a good conclusion to any important exercise (especially one that required prolonged effort and commitment from the horse), since it lets the horse free his back and relax the muscles that contributed the most to his work. His willingness to do this is also a sign that his posture during the exercise was correct (see illustration).

Working "long and low."

Mistakes When Working Long and Low

Mistakes by the Rider

– Letting go of the reins entirely and losing the contact with the horse's mouth instead of accompanying the descent of the head correctly (this allows the horse to lose all momentum).
– Leaning forward as the horse lowers or extends his head.
– Failing to keep the horse moving forward with engagement (the lowering of the neck shouldn't change the gait the horse is working in).

Mistakes by the Horse

– Rushing (this usually means the shoulders are overloaded; you need to slow the horse down and let him rebalance, and then try again).
– Losing energy (this means you need to encourage a little more impulsion).
– Dropping the contact (this means you should slow down, then very gradually resume a working pace).
– Pulling the reins from the rider's hands (this is a defensive action, and you'll need to figure out why the horse thinks he has to do it before you can fix it; it may also be an indication that he's been uncomfortable or unbalanced and you didn't notice).

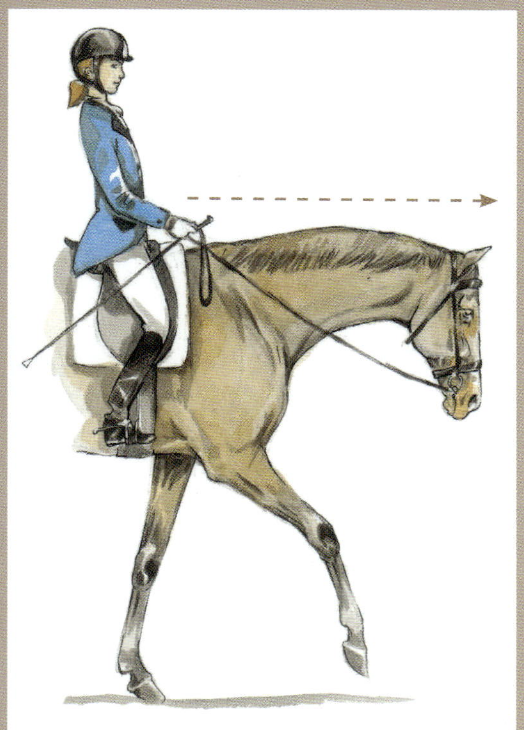
Working with the neck extended but not lowered.

To ask your horse to extend his neck, first, close your legs, in order to slightly increase his impulsion (without going to the point of imbalance); then gradually open your fingers without letting him lower his head (vibrating your reins lightly). Your horse will then extend his head himself.

The contact with his mouth should remain consistent, and you should have the feeling that you could choose to interrupt this movement at any moment.

Working with the neck extended is beneficial:
– It allows "the horse to immediately give his entire front end the length and degree of extension called for to develop his gait."[55]
– It's a good way to check whether your horse's way of going is correct. A tense or constrained horse (whose way of going is impaired) will extend his head upward, not forward, when he's released by the opening of the rider's fingers. By contrast, the horse whose posture and bearing are correct will extend forward, seeking the contact.
– Because it extends the horse's topline, it allows:[56]

- The horse's center of gravity to drop lower and move forward, which alters the horse's balance in a way that favors even greater lengthening. This makes it possible to strengthen the horse's natural impulsion and ensure that he moves his legs with lightness with significantly less effort by the rider.
- The horse to adopt a way of going that lets him carry the rider with greater energy (stretching and lifting his back).
- The horse and rider to practice keeping the horse on the bit and "in the hands" from the very first lessons—in a state of balance that encourages forward movement, with a relaxed topline and a flexible and mobile neck, basic contact is usually enough. The horse won't react defensively to counter the rider, and the head/neck angle will gradually close as the horse begins to lift his neck and collect himself.

33

To request a lowered neck, you simply open your fingers progressively around your reins, and lower your hands, yielding with your legs while keeping your calves in gentle contact (to maintain momentum). If your approach is correct, your horse will extend his neck and drop the tip of his nose forward and down (if not, he'll straighten his head and speed up). All you have to do is follow this movement of his head, letting the reins slide as much as necessary.

Working with the Neck Extended

At a lively trot, caress the neck on the right and then on the left, without letting go of the reins; this is one way to get an extension of the neck.

Nuno Oliveira

The extension of the neck is an elongation horizontally, with the head moving away from the body *without* descending toward the ground the way it does when you work "long and low."

. Working on uphill and downhill slopes is excellent exercise for the horse.

– Depending on the way it's done (with the head lower or higher, or more extended or less extended, and the intensity of the work done), it can help compensate for or even correct minor faults in conformation—relaxing and lengthening a short neck, for example, or rounding an inverted neck.

This exercise is worth practicing at the walk and trot, in particular, and is a very good relaxation for the horse when trotting him outside the arena. You can also use it at the canter, but keep in mind that since it helps loosen and supple the topline, it can alter the horse's balance (and thus put him on his forehand). It shouldn't be done with horses who have any issues with navicular syndrome, since it encourages the horse to transfer weight to his forelegs.

Working on a Slope

It's outdoors, facing natural obstacles, where the rider [can] acquire a feel for the canter stride, impulsion, and the straightness of the horse.

Nuno Oliveira

Working on a slope (uphill or downhill) is an excellent way to soften, supple, and ultimately relax the horse. Going uphill strengthens the hindquarters and increases their thrust and impulsion, and works the back (in much the same way the extended gaits do); going downhill encourages the horse to lower his hips and step under himself with his hindquarters (in much the same way the collected gaits do) in order to keep his balance.

This kind of work will be all the more effective if you do it at walk and at trot, in a rhythm similar to the way your horse moves in each gait on the flat. Whether you're taking him uphill or downhill, don't let him speed up or slow down; ask him to maintain the regularity of his gait. The movement of his neck (as when he's extending or collecting himself) will let him manage the energy of his steps in this type of exercise.

This is hard work for the horse, and it asks a lot of him; don't overdo it, and incorporate frequent rest periods on level ground, with long reins.

· The rider to avoid causing the horse's back to turn "hollow," even in the most sustained stretches.

– It's an excellent gymnastic approach for show jumping, because it rounds the horse from the tip of his nose to his tail.

– It stretches the entire spine, in alignment, which improves the lateral flexibility of the horse (since he can then bend with his entire body).

34

Mistakes When Working with the Neck Extended
Mistakes by the Rider
The same as for Working "Long and Low" (see page 32)
Mistakes by the Horse
– Opening the angle of the neck and head too far (this collapses the base of the neck and the topline; you'll need to get the horse back on the bit and "in your hands," and then start again more gradually). – Lifting the neck (same as above). – Failing to open the angle of the neck and head enough (this means you need to work on teaching your horse to seek the contact when you loosen your hands on the reins).

Working in Canter and Counter-Canter

The canter is a series of three leaps; each leap contains the next leap.

Nuno Oliveira

Before discussing work at counter-canter and its many virtues, let's revisit a few points about cantering the horse correctly in general. Working on the canter, in dressage, is an exacting task.[57] It comes in three stages: *strengthening it, straightening it,* and *collecting it.*

Strengthening the Canter

"The first goal to strive for with gymnastic exercises at canter is steadiness of foot—that is to say, maintaining order and rhythm in the sequence of the horse's footfalls and the movements of his limbs, whatever the demands of the work may be."[58] It's a question of seeking balance and regularity in the gait.

To help you achieve this, you should practice the following exercises, in this order:
– Longeing.
– Cantering outside the arena.
– Cantering on circles, bent to the outside,[59] to give energy to the forehand and emphasize the horse's inside hind leg—and then the same thing but on straight lines, if the horse is in balance.
– Counter-canter work—broken lines, then 20-meter semicircles, and then serpentines with three loops.

Straightening the Canter

This work can be done at the same time as work on collecting the canter, and, unsurprisingly, the aim is to increase straightness—to help the horse move smoothly and symmetrically, which will develop his musculature and give him greater impulsion and better balance. Straightening the canter must be done pro-

This horse is perfectly straight: the shoulders are in front of the hips.

35

gressively, gradually, working on circles and repositioning the shoulders to put them in front of the hips at each stride, in shoulder-fore and counter-canter on both leads.

Collecting the Canter

The earliest beginnings of collection involve lowering the hips and preparing the horse to collect himself more fully. Work on this with repeated canter departs, close together, in balance, from the walk; counter-canter on increasingly tight curves; asking for counter-canter departs on circles; and working in haunches-in.

Counter-Canter

A horse is in **counter-canter** when he's turning to the side opposite the lead he's cantering on—for example, cantering on the right lead while traveling on a curve to the left. In the progression of a horse's dressage training, the counter-canter only comes into play once a horse is already responsive and able to maintain his cadence well in true canter, and able to strike off without hesitation on either lead.

Counter-canter has many benefits if it's practiced with an eye to the horse's balance and rhythm:
– It encourages the hindquarters to engage.
– It promotes greater mobility in the outside shoulder.
– It favors a more collected, uphill balance than cantering normally.
– In general, it improves and refines the balance of the horse, his roundness, and his feel in the contact.

To use counter-canter successfully, the horse must not break his rhythm when transitioning from canter to counter-canter—there must be no disruption in the horse's overall balance, either front-to-back (as seen in the horse who "dives" into counter-canter) or lateral (as seen in the horse who falls onto the outside shoulder).

> To counter-canter, you must maintain the aids of the canter depart and then work each stride as if it were a new stride in the canter. The counter-canter therefore becomes a series of canter departs.

Stages of Practicing the Counter-Canter

– Zigzag half-passes, first deviating very little from the track, and then gradually increasing in duration until you're half-passing from the track to the centerline.
– Half-voltes, large enough on the short side to allow the horse to find his balance before approaching the curve. Your first few half-voltes will be very wide, but as you keep working on them, you'll be able to tighten them and bring them closer and closer to the short side, increasing their difficulty.
– Changing rein along the diagonal (away from the corners, when you first start to try this).
– Counter-canter on large circles, gradually decreasing their diameter.
– Figures of eight, with the horse alternating between canter and counter-canter—with his rhythm, balance, and suppleness remaining unchanged.

Challenges for the Rider

– The very fact of counter-canter—maintaining the same rhythm and quality of gait in the counter-canter as in the canter.
– The necessity of guiding the horse, having to follow a precise route while keeping the horse in counter-canter.

Staying in counter-canter and preventing the horse from changing leads or losing coordination, it's essential to keep the same position and feel you have when you're cantering. Most counter-canters fail because the rider tenses up or shifts her weight, which means the position and the function of the aids she's trying to apply change the moment the horse transitions to counter-canter.

Riding counter-canter on a curve, whether the second loop of a serpentine or a 20-meter half-circle, you have to know exactly where you want to go. Direct your gaze and your chest in the direction you want to ride, and mentally visualize the curve you're going to make before you even get there, as if it were an obstacle course. From the first loop of your serpentine, or before your counter-canter half-circle, pay attention to the cadence of your horse's gait and keep your gaze aimed where you want to go. Then direct your horse on each stride, bringing his shoulders to the correct path.

Success with the counter-canter also depends on the quality of the true canter, and your ability to help the horse maintain this quality while you're riding curves in counter-canter. If the horse's canter isn't very good, then the counter-canter will be even worse. So you have to take care of your canter first.

For the successful counter-canter, your horse must be in balance and on the bit, as a result of:

– **Your seat**, which ensures your stability in the saddle.
– **Your legs**, which help the horse maintain his momentum.
– **Your hands**, which regulate his impulsion and preserve your soft contact with his mouth.
– **Your torso**, which needs to be straight and upright.

It's often a change in the seat or bearing of the rider (who unintentionally blocks the horse, stiffens up, or moves her aids) at the start of a counter-canter arena figure that causes a change in the horse's way of going.

Avoid bending the neck too much (to the left when the horse is on the left lead, for example); the ideal is for the neck to remain almost straight, in fact, so you can help the horse maintain his lateral balance.

The canter is effectively a succession of "leaps." You have to balance yourself in order to balance your horse. On a curve ridden in counter-canter, keep yourself balanced and you'll make it much easier for your horse to balance himself; just keep your aids steady, in the same place and with the same feel you use in the canter.

Mistakes in the Counter-Canter

Mistakes by the Rider

– Speeding up or slowing down the motion of the pelvis (you must keep following the horse's motion the same way you were following it in the canter).
– Changing the position of the legs (this will disrupt the horse's motion and potentially cause him to change leads).

Mistakes by the Horse

– Failing to maintain the gait—dropping back to a trot, and then returning to canter.
– Changing leads (bring him to a halt and then resume the counter-canter).
– Losing his balance, either front-to-back or laterally (either the canter that preceded the counter-canter wasn't balanced correctly to begin with, or you accidentally changed your bearing on his back or shifted your weight).

37

A rider counter-cantering on the right lead (the horse is cantering on the right lead while tracking left).

The horse is straight when he keeps his rhythm, when he isn't heavier in the hand on one side than on the other, and when, starting on the centerline, he can readily strike off into a 6-meter volte to the right or to the left with equal ease.

Nuno Oliveira

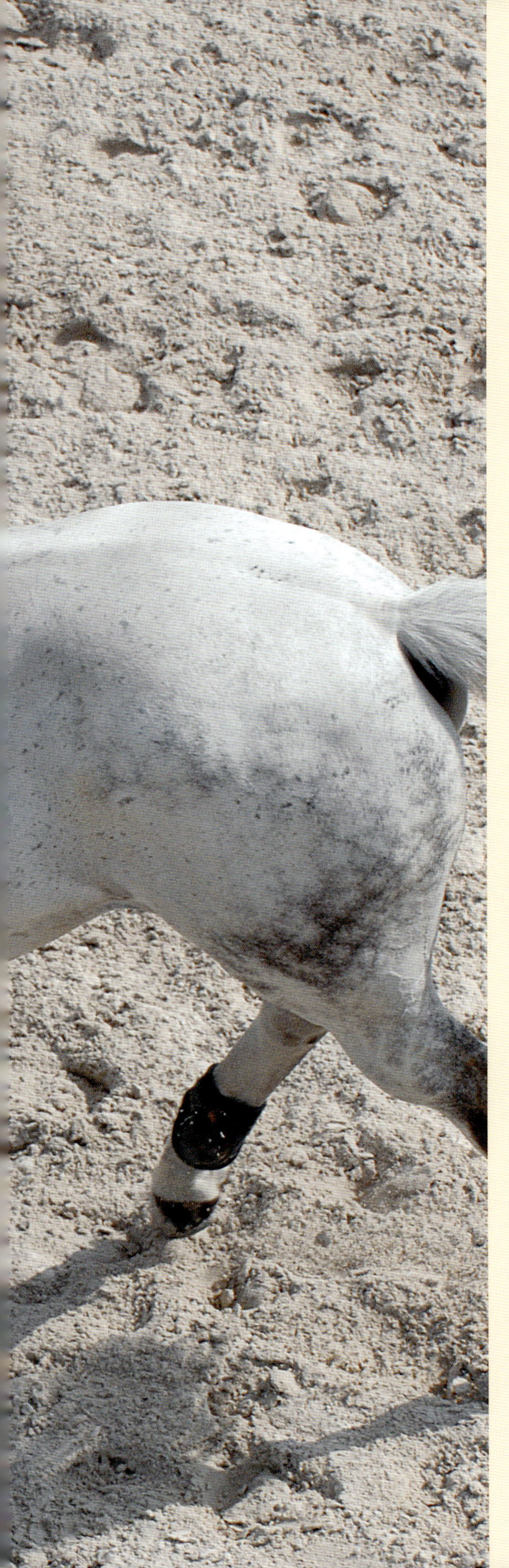

Working on a Circle and Other Arena Figures

Straightness

Horses, like human beings, are born either "right-handed" or "left-handed," so to speak. This means a horse is naturally more flexible on one side than the other; you'll have an easier time getting him to bend in one direction, and it'll be harder to bend him in the other. If he's "right-handed," then you'll have trouble bringing his head to the right, since that means stretching his stiffer and less flexible left side. If he's "left-handed," you'll have trouble bringing the head around to the left, and he may feel like he's pulling to the left but rarely tightens the right rein.

Further observation will show you that "right-handedness" in a horse[60] (for example) has a number of persistent consequences:

For the Horse

The horse will default to a way of going in which the hips will tend to shift slightly to the right of the shoulders.

The left hind leg will tend to reach farther under the horse and is inclined to bend but not inclined to push off strongly; the right hind

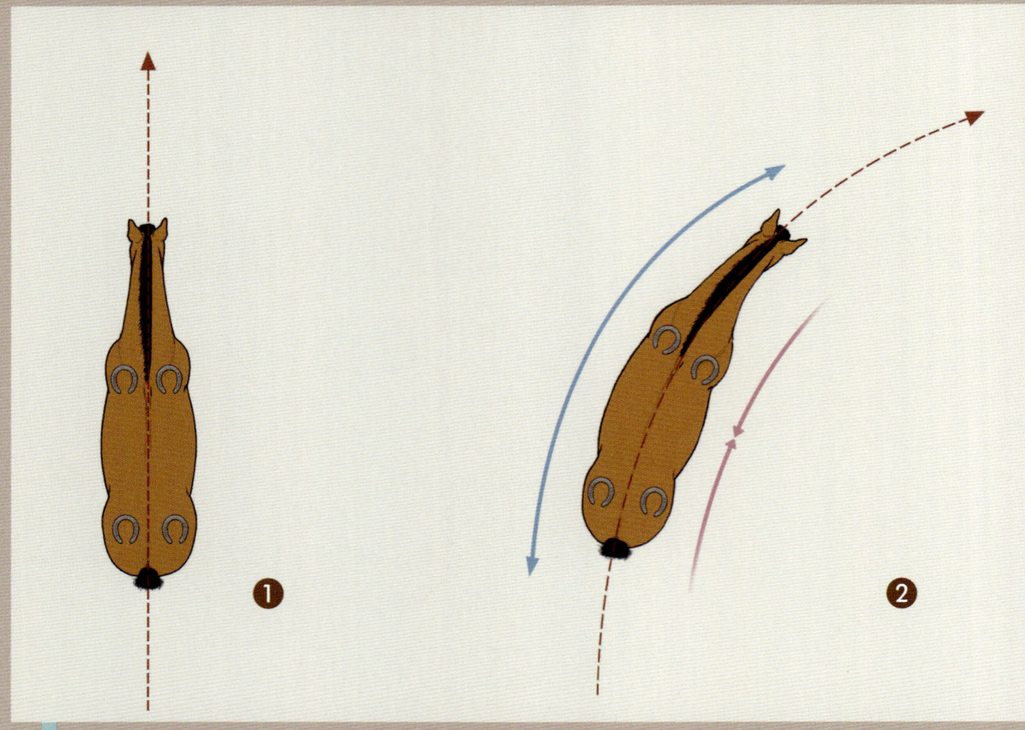

The ultimate goal of dressage is the straight horse (1). To achieve this, working on a curve (2) is necessary, to stretch the muscles to the outside and strengthen the muscles to the inside of the bend.

leg is less engaged and is inclined to push off strongly but not to bend.

The left side will be "shorter" and more difficult to stretch and relax; the right side will be "long." This results in:

– More dynamic thrust from the right hind leg; the typical example is the horse who, when he jumps, tends to shift consistently to the left (thanks to the tendency of the right hind to push more strongly than the left hind).

– A ready tendency to bend to the left, and difficulty bending to the right.

– A tendency for the horse to lose engagement when he's bent to the left (whether on a circle, in shoulder-in, or in half-pass).[61]

– A tendency for the horse to struggle with bending and "run away" from the exercise by speeding up when he's bent to the right (whether on a circle, in shoulder-in, or in half-pass).[62]

– A noticeable difference between the horse's extension from a right shoulder-in (very good) and from a left shoulder-in (not so much).

For the Rider

The rider will get the feeling that her horse "isn't pushing straight." She may also have the impression that the horse doesn't particularly care about one rein (the left rein, in our example of a horse who's "right-handed") but "pulls" on the other (the right)—because the right side of his body moves more freely, he would prefer to stretch that side, and hold his head to the left, rather than hold his head to the right and have to extend that stiffer left side.

When the rider is maintaining identical degrees of contact with both reins, the horse will still be holding his head to the left.

High-quality training should make it possible to gradually correct these tendencies; straightness in the horse is one of the primary objectives of dressage.

When a horse moves with perfect straightness, his hind legs are in exact alignment with his forelegs.[63] He uses all his strength, all his power, to achieve the movement the rider is asking for, and the rider will have full control of that movement, with the horse fully "in her hands."[64] When the horse is crooked, by contrast, some impulsion will always "leak" out one shoulder or the other. Straightness allows all the horse's impulsion to be used in collection, without "losing" any of it.

General L'Hotte wrote that straightness begins with "honesty" in the horse's forward movement. This means that a straight horse, above all, must be in front of the leg (but not rushing away from the leg and upsetting his own balance). Straightness is a bit like rolling a hula hoop in front of you; the slower you go, the more unsteady the hoop is, and the more it will tend to tip. Rolling it forward with energy, though, will help it stay upright and keep its line of travel straighter. However, you can't send it rolling away too fast, or you won't be able to keep up with it to make sure it continues rolling in the right direction.

Canter on the right lead, on a circle to the right in a show jumping competition.

41

> "The horse is straight when the hind feet line up exactly with the hoofprints left by the front feet; it follows that the hips and shoulders are also lined up, which ensures that the biomechanical interplay between them is correct. With both hips working equally, impulsion is equally distributed, and the horse's weight shifts smoothly and easily."
>
> Général L'Hotte

In practice, the horse being straight and correctly aligned on the axis of his movement:
– Ensures the even distribution of his weight, through the action of his hips.
– Helps preserve the horse's physical health, because it means both sides of his body are being worked equally and reduces strain on his joints and muscles over the long term.
– Makes his full physical power available to the rider, without tension, wasted effort, or unnecessary movement.

It's through work on curved lines, sequences of arena figures, and work on two tracks that you'll begin to achieve straightness. Work on a circle allows you to straighten your horse over the entire length of his body—by keeping him on the aids around a curve, you bend him "from head to tail." In doing so, you invite him to contract to the inside and stretch to the outside.[65]

Straightness and bend are inseparable. But for bending the horse on curved lines to lead to straightness, it must lengthen the "stiff" side without stiffening the "long" side; it needs to soften rather than cause strain, which would only create tension, reduce your horse's available strength, and make him less responsive to your aids. To return to the example of the "right-handed" horse, this horse would need progressive stretches for his left side in order to maintain contact with the bit on his left.

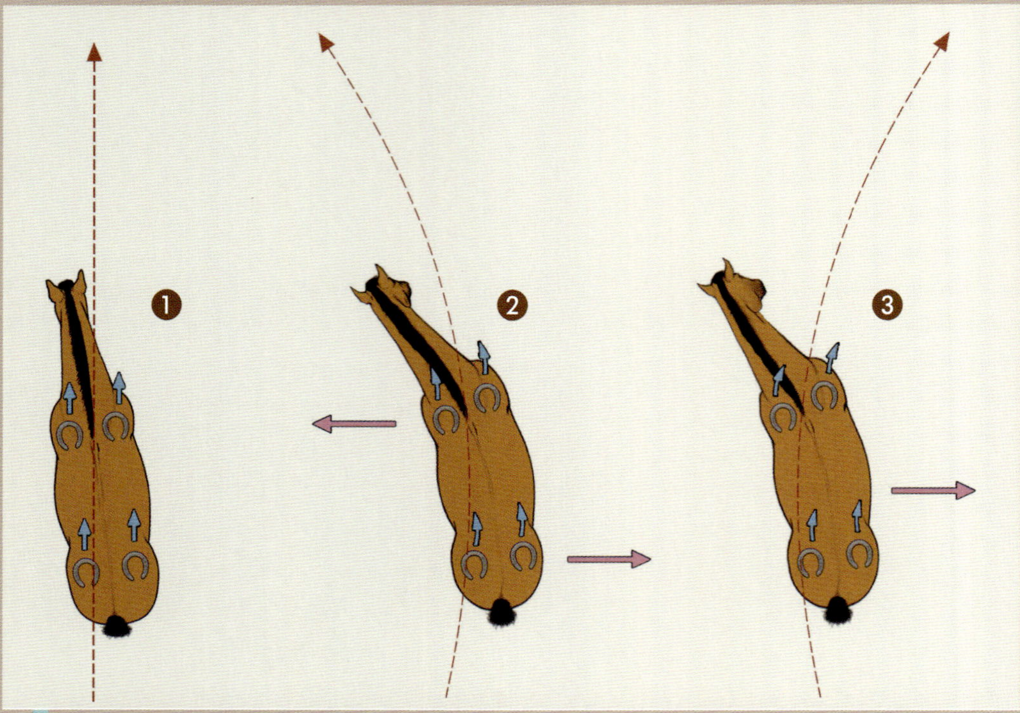

The horse is naturally asymmetrical. It seems to be more common for horses to be "right-handed"—to like to hold their necks to the left and bend to the left, stretching their more flexible right side on the outside of the bend, instead of their less flexible left side (1). On a circle to the left (2), the problem gets worse, which causes the horse to fall onto his left shoulder and sends his hips to the right. On a circle to the right (3), the horse is counter-bent and tends to fall toward the inside of the circle.

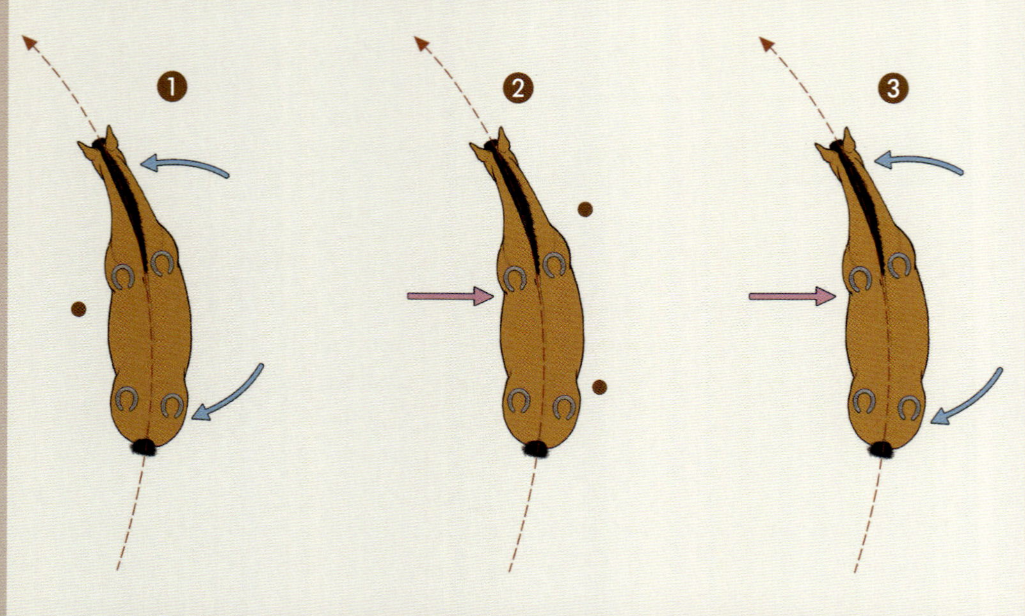

The rider can bend the horse by bending the "ends" around the middle (1), by pushing "through" the middle (2), or by combining the two (3).

Once his stiff side has softened, he'll stop resisting on the right, since he'll no longer be uncomfortable bending to the right and stretching that left side.

In practice, a horse's natural asymmetry can be reduced, but doesn't truly disappear. "The rider, with all the perfection of her art, spends her life correcting this imperfection."[66] At the beginning of dressage training, or when working with a young horse, straightness will be limited to walking on a straight line in a given direction.

Circles and Curved Lines

On a circle, make sure the horse doesn't weight his inside shoulder. Your seat should have even contact on both sides. On a circle, stay with the bend of the horse: move the outside shoulder forward.

Nuno Oliveira

The purpose of working on curved lines is to make the line of the horse's spine match the bend of the figure you're riding; you must therefore bend your horse with an eye to aligning him with the circumference of the circle.

Bend is defined as "the lateral curvature of the spine, obtained through the action of the rider's aids." It's correct only if it's even, regular, and doesn't create tension along the topline. This last is fundamental—it demonstrates that bend hasn't been forced[67] and that the circumference of the circle isn't too tight a curve for your horse's current level of ability.

To bend your horse, you can:
– "Push" the horse's head and tail to follow the line of the circle while maintaining the position of the horse's core (acting from the outside toward the inside with your outside lateral aids, while the resistance of your inside leg creates a barrier in the middle).
– Keep the horse's head and tail on the line of the circle and "push" the middle of the horse (acting from the inside toward the outside with your inside leg, while your outside lateral aids create a barrier at the front and the back).

In practice, a combination of both methods is the most effective. The aids for creating bend this way are as follows (for a circle to the left, for example):
– The left rein opens to bring the tip of the horse's nose inward; at more advanced levels of dressage training, the inside hand, always lower than the outside hand, determines the precise position of the horse's muzzle.
– The outside rein gives way to allow the horse to turn his head, and then controls the movement of the shoulders; at more advanced levels of dressage training, the outside hand, always held higher, determines the precise height of the neck. It's this same hand that's responsible for adjusting the horse if his frame changes, and that regulates his speed by controlling his outside shoulder.

The two reins frame the neck. Your gaze should be pointed in the direction you want to go, because this will naturally orient your chest and shoulders correctly. Your shoulders will be parallel to the horse's, with your inside shoulder slightly behind and your outside shoulder slightly forward.
– The rider's inside leg stays at the girth. It's the leg around which the horse is curving himself. It's also the leg responsible for the horse's impulsion.
– The rider's outside leg moves back, independently. It controls the horse's hips and keeps the hindquarters on the circle, and is also responsible for the activity of the horse's outside hind leg.

Both legs frame the horse's body. Your hips should be parallel to the horse's hips.
– Your weight, if it moves at all, should be oriented in the direction of the movement (this is a good rule no matter what movement you're doing).[68] Ideally, your weight should be equally balanced across your seat bones; however, when you're riding across a circle, your balance might shift slightly inward.

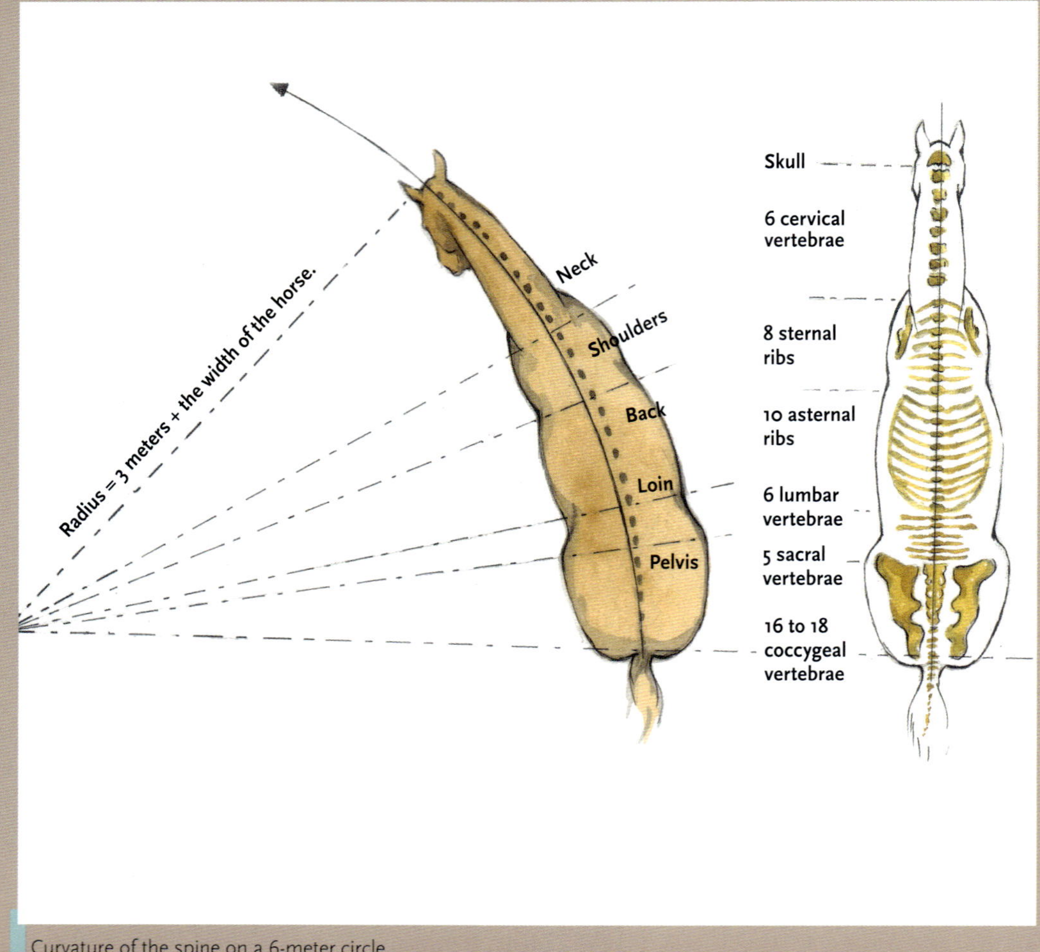

Curvature of the spine on a 6-meter circle.

One of the most common mistakes when working on a circle is trying to bend the horse too much. This often results in the horse's neck bending too far to the inside, and the outside shoulder or outside hip "falling out."

Remember that on a 20-meter circle, the bend you need in the horse is minimal. The amount of bend is only really going to become obvious on a circle that's 15 meters or smaller.

Your aids should form a corridor through which your horse is moving; they shouldn't be a constraint that "pins" him in place on the circle and constricts his movement. Riding on a circle should *feel* flexible, with the horse moving correctly: you should be able to tell he's maneuver-

The circle is used to assess the maturity of the rider and the level of training of a dressage horse. If this is the first arena figure you learn with your horse, that means it's the one you'll always find yourself coming back to.

ing with his forelegs, adjusting the bend in his body to the circumference of the circle. As his body becomes increasingly supple and relaxed, you can reduce the size of the circle. The smaller it is, the greater the difficulty of the exercise.

Finally, keep in mind that an 8-meter circle requires the horse to be capable of collected gaits; the smallest circle typically ridden in training is a 6-meter volte.

Work on the circle begins with practicing riding corners correctly: "Riding a corner correctly involves several elements: impulsion on a straight line, and the beginning of a correct circle or shoulder-in."[69]

Riding a corner is the first step in working on bend more generally, because it forces you to find your balance on the horse when he's bent around your inside leg, and it allows you to adjust his self-carriage with the aids. To keep his balance, impulsion, and rhythm through a corner, your horse will need to do extra work flexing and pushing off with his inside hind leg; this means that your job as the rider is to keep him on the aids, active, and bent around your inside leg.

This is only possible if you're paying close attention to balance, impulsion, and rhythm with each of your horse's strides—and taking extra care when approaching a change of direction (so your horse isn't surprised by the action of an aid at the last moment).

A good circle:
– Is round and composed of two identical half-circles. (It seems obvious, and yet...!) Where you're looking, your visualization of the route you want to take (the same way you'd visualize your approach to a jump), and paying attention to your reference points (B and X, for example) are all essential.
– Is precisely placed within the arena. If you're riding a circle at B, then it's at B, not a stride before or a stride past B.
– Is performed at an even, regular gait. Whether you're moving from a straight line into a circle, or you're on the circle, or you're moving out of the circle and back onto a straight line, the horse

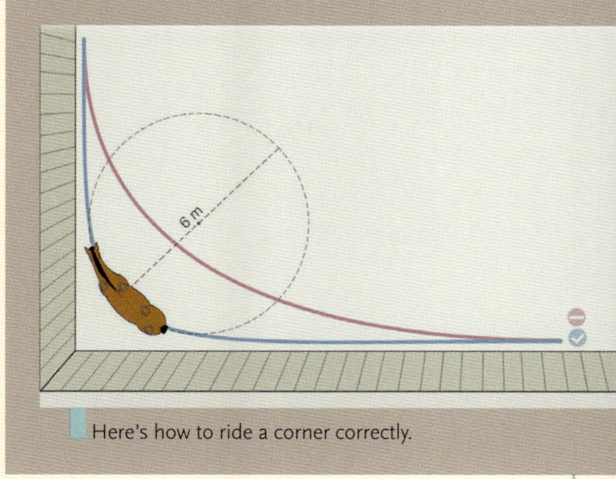
Here's how to ride a corner correctly.

must maintain the same walk, the same trot, the same canter—the same speed and rhythm.

To perform a good circle, you must be able to control the three fundamentals: balance, the approach, and the turn.

The most common mistakes by the rider on a circle:
– Using too much inside hand to create the bend (this often creates too much bend, and risks causing the outside shoulder to fall out).
– Shifting the shoulders sideways too much or too little (this affects the bend and will make the circle wobbly or uneven).
– Riding the circle with a stiff torso, or with the shoulders at the wrong angle (same as above).
– Riding the circle with an uneven seat (this will result in your weight shifting to the outside).
– Failing to use the inside leg at the girth correctly (holding it stiffly, positioning it incorrectly, or using it too hesitantly), or having the horse fail to respond to it (this will lead the horse to bend only his forehand instead of his whole body).
– Failing to coordinate the aids correctly, or having the horse fail to respond to them (this will lead to the horse contracting his neck and failing to stretch the outside of his body properly).
– Failing to use the aids correctly in general (this will lead to an incorrect position and the horse's neck "breaking" to the inside).

> Work on the circle provides the rider with the means and opportunity to control the movements of the horse's inside hind leg—to prevent it from escaping sideways and to engage it under the horse's center of gravity.
> Decarpentry

<table>
<tr><th colspan="2" align="center">Mistakes by the Horse on a Circle</th></tr>
<tr>
<td rowspan="2">Shoulders falling to the outside.</td>
<td>You may be pulling too much on the inside rein.</td>
</tr>
<tr>
<td>Your horse may be:
– Unbalanced on the forehand (usually because he's going too fast, so you should slow him down using the outside rein).
– Lacking in impulsion and therefore "behind" your leg (so you should close your legs and channel his movement forward with the outside rein).
(In both cases, there's probably an issue with your horse's balance relative to his impulsion.)</td>
</tr>
<tr>
<td rowspan="2">The horse falling to the inside, or being counterflexed.</td>
<td>You may be drawing the outside rein toward yourself, instead of keeping it to the side to support the horse on the circle.</td>
</tr>
<tr>
<td>Your horse may:
– Be unbalanced on the forehand (usually because he's going too fast; slow him down, and then ask him to bend again).
– Lack impulsion and therefore be "behind" your leg (so you should close your legs to ask his inside hind leg to engage, and open your outside rein to encourage his shoulders to move toward the outside of the circle, which should bring them into alignment and restore his straightness).
(In both cases, there's probably an issue with your horse's balance relative to his impulsion.)
– Need you to ask him to bend to the inside.
– Need a reminder to respond to your inside leg aid.</td>
</tr>
<tr>
<td rowspan="2">Haunches falling to the inside.</td>
<td>You may be using your outside leg too much.</td>
</tr>
<tr>
<td>Your horse may not be moving with enough forward energy (so you should open your fingers around the reins, close your legs, or both).</td>
</tr>
<tr>
<td rowspan="2">Haunches falling to the outside.</td>
<td>Your inside leg may be too far back (you need to keep it at the girth).</td>
</tr>
<tr>
<td>Your horse may be off-balance, on his outside shoulder, or going too fast (so you should slow him down and channel the energy of his hips with your outside leg).</td>
</tr>
<tr>
<td rowspan="2">Rushing around the circle.</td>
<td>He may be falling to the inside.</td>
</tr>
<tr>
<td>Straighten him—usually opening the outside rein will put his shoulders in the right place again—and then ask him to bend again.</td>
</tr>
<tr>
<td rowspan="2">Losing impulsion.</td>
<td>He may be "leaking" through his outside shoulder.</td>
</tr>
<tr>
<td>Close your legs to encourage greater activity in his hindquarters.</td>
</tr>
<tr>
<td>Dropping his shoulders.</td>
<td>Straighten him—usually opening the outside rein will put his shoulders in the right place again—and then ask him to bend again.</td>
</tr>
</table>

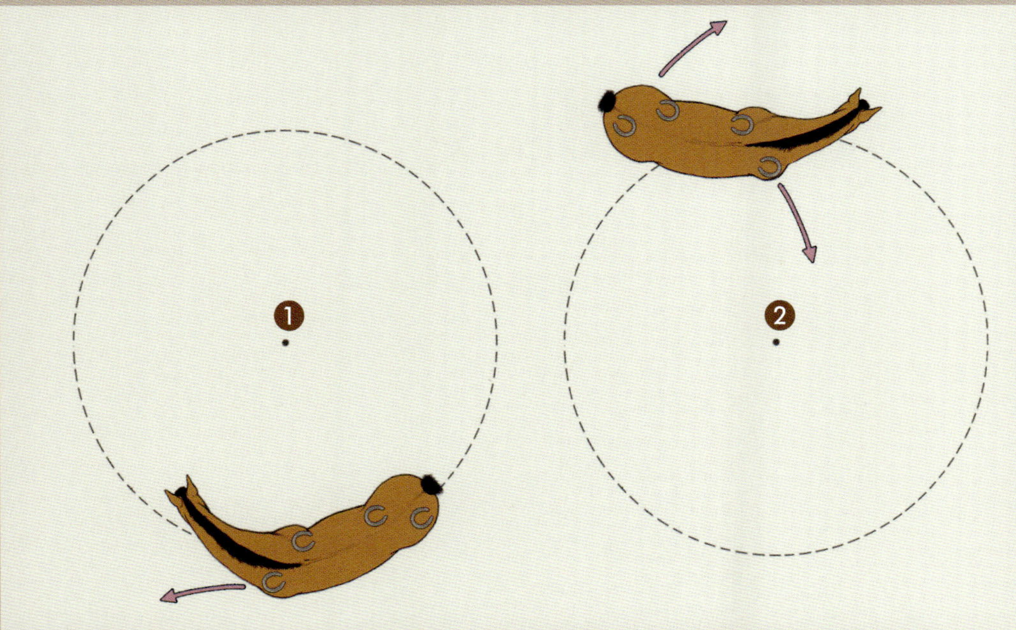

Two classic mistakes on the circle: (1) too much bend, with the shoulders falling out, and (2) the horse counter-flexing and falling to the inside (with the hips falling out).

A circle at canter on the right lead: the horse is dropping his shoulders on the circle.

Serpentines and Figure Eights

During voltes and serpentines, make sure the horse keeps the same contact on both reins; this is the proof that his neck hasn't "broken." The serpentine is a valuable exercise for working on "feel"; you must be able to tell whether there's more resistance on any one loop than on the others.

Nuno Oliveira

Serpentines and figure eights complement work on a circle by softening the horse in both directions alternately. The number of loops you can fit into your serpentines is going to depend on the flexibility of your horse; the more flexible he becomes, the more loops you can do (3, 4, 5 …). The most important part of this work is still the quality of the horse's movement—his suppleness, balance, and way of going should be maintained throughout, and proof of your success in these respects will come in the consistency of his cadence.

In general, changing the direction of the horse's bend will make any problem you're already having on the circle, as described in the previous section,[70] more obvious (both in the moment as you ride, and from a training perspective as you work on these figures). That's why it's typically recommended that you approach riding these figures gradually. You should take your time, and that will make it easier to understand the issues you're facing and keep your horse supple, balanced, and rhythmic in his movements.

The sequence in transitioning from a curve to the left to a curve to the right, as an example, might be as follows:

– Ride with a left bend, with your horse on the aids for the left bend.

– Shift your aids to symmetrical positions to allow your horse to straighten himself.

– After a few strides, position your aids for a right bend.

Serpentine at the trot: a loop to the right.

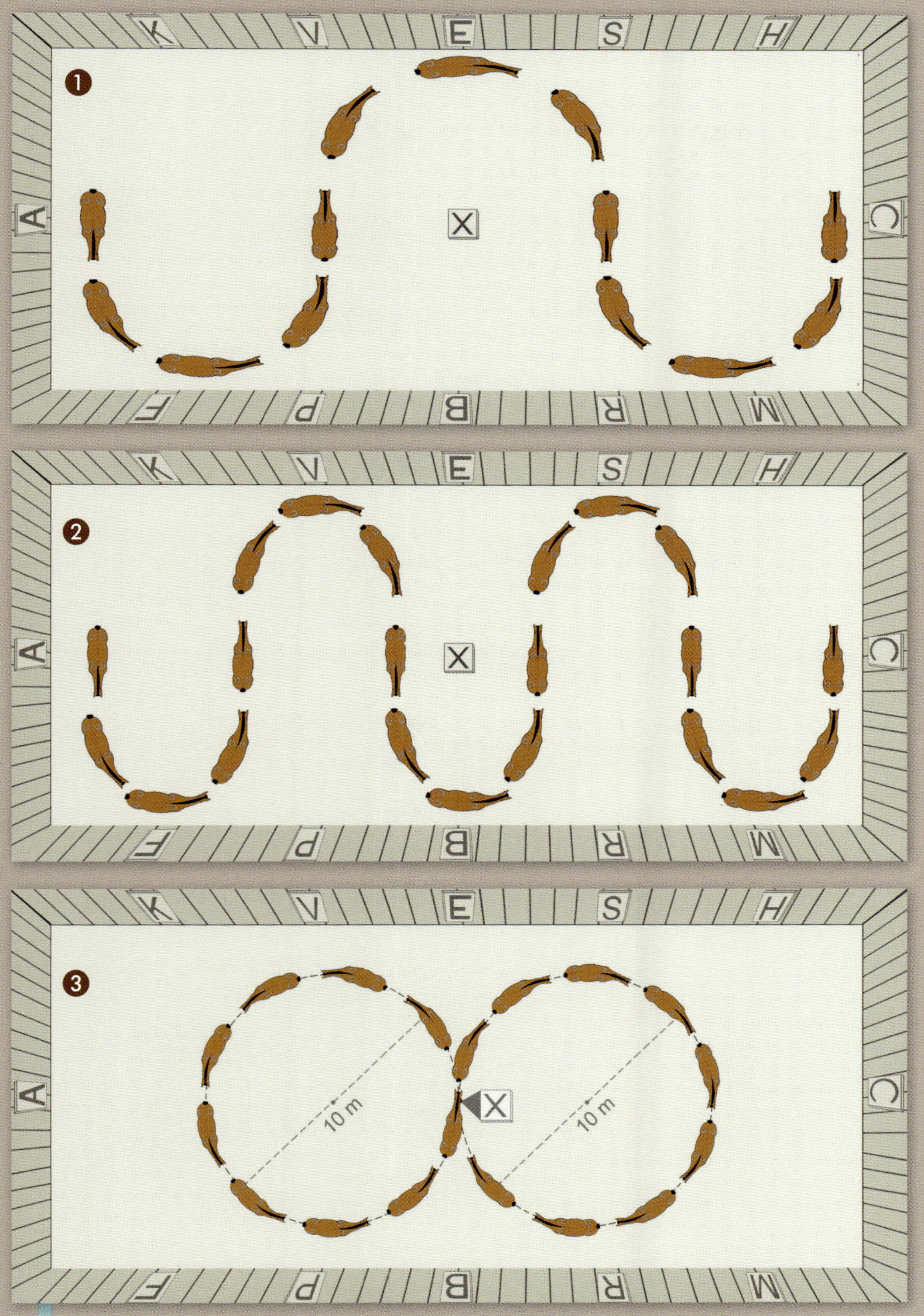

You can vary the number of loops in a serpentine from 3 (1) to 5 (2), or more, depending on the size of the space you're working in, but the loops must be consistent with each other—that's where the difficulty in the exercise lies. 3. A figure eight at X.

– Let your horse move into the "corridor" of your aids and bend to the right for the turn.

Remember to "sink" into your saddle as deeply as you can, in order to make yourself as steady, as fixed, and as precise as possible in the use of your aids.

Relaxation Exercises on a Circle

If a young horse does a simple job well, know how to appreciate his willingness; if an old horse overcomes his stiffness to satisfy you, know how to appreciate that, too.

Nuno Oliveira

The Four Basic Exercises

Relaxation exercises based on the circle consist of changing the work the horse is doing, on a large circle or the curved part of a half-circle, by changing the degree of bend in his neck, the bend in his body, and the placement of his hindquarters.

So you can work:
– Bending to the inside, keeping the haunches to the outside of the circle (which favors work on the shoulders, and softens the inside hind leg) (1).
– Bending to the outside, keeping the haunches to the inside (working the outside hind leg) (2).
– Bending to the outside, keeping the haunches to the outside (counter-bending) (3).
– Bending to the inside, keeping the haunches to the inside (working in the same direction as the bend) (4).

Practiced in this order, these four exercises encourage the engagement of one hind leg, and then the other, and confirm the contact on one side, and then the other. Done in each di-

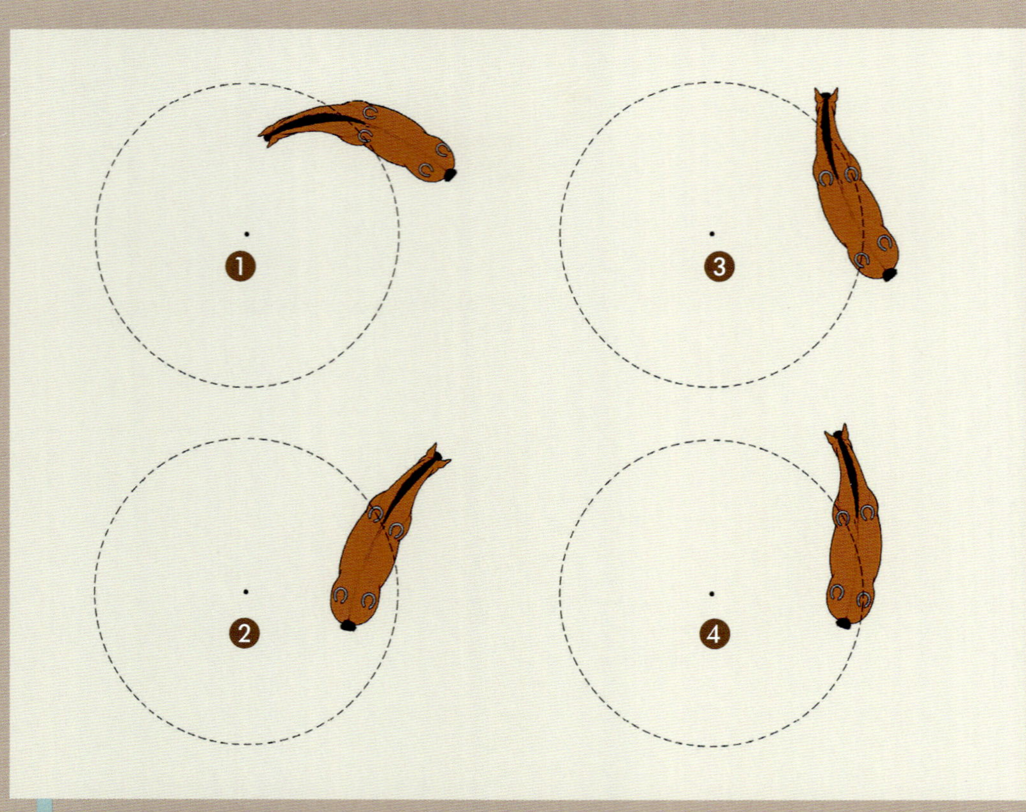

The four basic exercises on the circle.

rection, they soften, stretch, and relax the horse; the horse will be straighter and more consistently on the bit,[71] when ridden in a straight line, and his hindquarters will engage with greater energy.

Put together, they form a reasonably complete whole, as long as they're performed in a spirit of forward movement but without haste, in relaxed calm, beginning at the walk and requesting each for only a few strides.

You'll know these exercises have been successful if:
– The horse can move through them in a state of relaxed calm, with impulsion but without haste.
– They can be performed without any change in the horse's gait, and with the rhythm of the gait remaining consistent throughout.
– On any given stride, you could ask for the exercise to end or you could ask the horse to continue, with equal ease.

The cadence and the quality of the gait should be a priority; if the horse freezes, trips, or rushes, that means that he isn't ready for the exercise yet, or If your horse's strides get a little shorter, that may be a sign that he's reaching a slightly more collected balance for himself; leave him to it, as long as he remains supple and relaxed. The aids for these exercises shouldn't be constraints—these are states of activity you can leave and return to gradually, depending on your horse's level of comfort.

You also need to be careful not to overdo it with these exercises. Do them four or five times during a training session—be precise about when you are and are not asking for them—and alternate them with long periods of walking or trotting with the reins long, where the horse is allowed to lower his head at least a few times. If your horse yanks his head down sharply (trying to relieve discomfort in his back), or gets "hot" during the exercise, it's a sign that you've asked too much and that it's time to move on to something else.

The great benefit with these exercises, apart from the way they stretch and relax your horse, is how they let you practice tact and lightness with

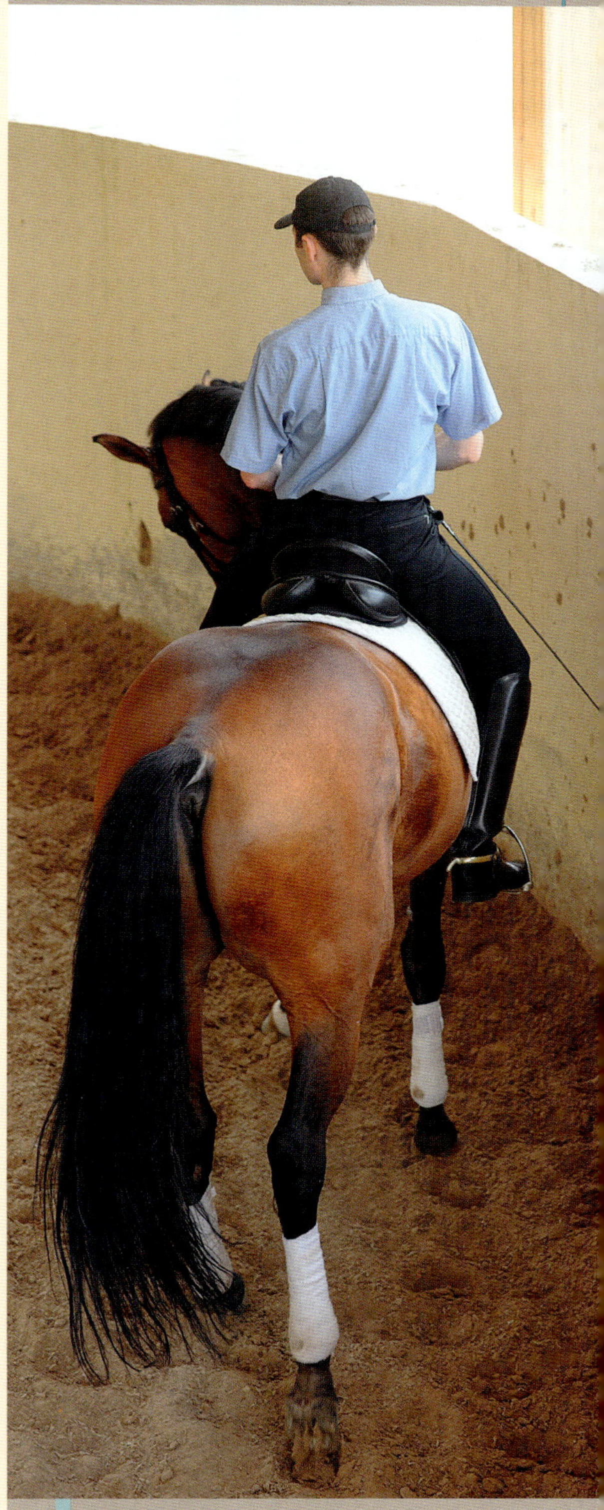

Working at a walk, in travers: bent to the inside, with the haunches kept to the inside.

your aids. In fact, performed at a walk, with the movement broken down into stages, they allow you to get familiar with the diagonal aids while remaining balanced (since you're at the walk) and in control of your horse's movements. They train you to feel your horse better, to tell when a movement has gone wrong so you can correct it.

1. Bent to the Inside, Haunches to the Outside
On the circle, maintaining bend to the inside, you move the haunches to the outside:
– First on one stride...
– ...then for several strides.

This exercise can be done in-hand[73] or under saddle, and encourages the horse to work through his shoulders and stretch his inside hind (which will be stepping in farther under his body); it also invites him to lower his neckline.

It should first be performed on a large circle (which you can gradually reduce to a 6-meter volte), or on a half-circle, and will become, when it's done on the spot, a half-turn on the forehand—the first step toward a reverse pirouette.[74] The smaller the circle, the more difficult the exercise becomes. For this exercise to be performed correctly, the inner hind leg has to step in under the horse's body and cross in front of the outer hind leg.

You can start by asking for this movement on a 16-meter circle around X.[75] This will give you a good reference point—one of the challenges of this exercise is getting the haunches to move to the outside without the shoulders leaving the track of the circle.

Step by Step
Starting from a circle to the left:
– Move the inside (left) hand wide to bring the tip of the horse's nose to the inside.
– Shift the inside (left) leg back, applying single-leg pressure to the horse's body.
– Slow the horse down slightly with pressure from the right rein, at the same time as your inside leg is acting.
– Encourage momentum (but not an increase in speed) with that inside leg.

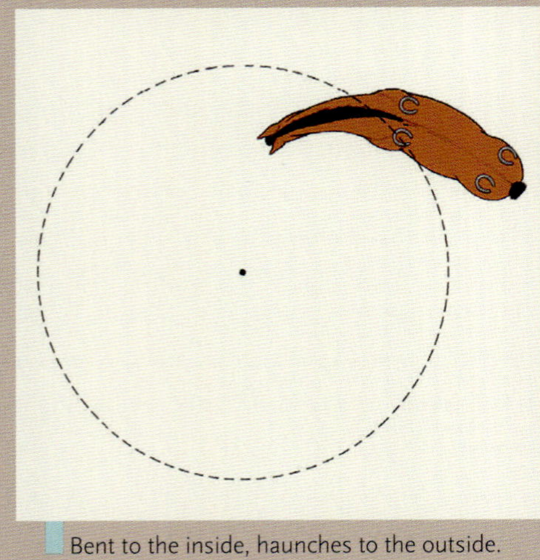
Bent to the inside, haunches to the outside.

– Feel your horse move his haunches to the outside of the circle (to the right), and release your aids to reward him.

You can then choose to stop, and allow your horse to return to his previous path around the circle, or repeat this sequence of aids to keep your horse's haunches out.

Either way, let the horse know you appreciate his efforts with a pat. Progress comes from frequent repetition of essential exercises—as long as they're alternated with periods of rest and relaxation.

To perform the exercise starting from a circle to the right, reverse the aids. Some points to keep in mind:

Common Mistakes with This Exercise

Mistakes by the Rider

– Coordinating the aids poorly, which means the rider can't successfully ask for the right movements from the horse, and also prevents her from dealing with any mistakes made or difficulties encountered by the horse.

Mistakes by the Horse

– Failing to stay on the track of the original circle, and making it bigger or smaller instead.
– Speeding up or slowing down.
– Losing his balance (this means you should try again at a slower gait, as that will make it easier for the horse to stay balanced).

– Make sure your horse's shoulders stay on the circle. The horse's track shouldn't change in such a way that the shoulders move in and the circle gets smaller (one of the most common mistakes that gets made with this exercise).

– Be careful not to ask for too deep of an angle. "Avoid an exaggerated movement of the haunches (a maximum of 30°–35°) that would kill the movement of the shoulders, which must precede the movement of the hindquarters."[76]

2. Bent to the Outside, Haunches to the Inside

On the circle, maintaining bend to the outside, you move the haunches inward for one or several strides.

This exercise, which follows the same logic as the previous one, can be practiced in-hand or under saddle. It encourages the horse to work through his shoulders and use his outside hind leg. It should first be performed on a large circle (which you can gradually reduce to a 6-meter volte), then in half-circles and finally in reverse half-circles. The smaller the circle, the more difficult this exercise becomes.

For this exercise to be executed correctly, the outer hind leg must step under the horse's body and cross in front of the inner hind leg.

You can start by asking for this movement on a 16-meter circle around X.[77] This will give you a good reference point—one of the challenges of this exercise is getting the haunches to move to the inside without the shoulders leaving the track of the circle.

Step by Step

Starting from a circle to the left:

– Move the outside (right) hand to bring the tip of the horse's nose to the outside.

– Shift the outside (right) leg back, applying single-leg pressure to the horse's body.

– Slow the horse down slightly with pressure from the left rein, at the same time as your outside leg is acting.

Bent to the outside, haunches to the inside.

– Encourage momentum (but not an increase in speed) with the inside (left) leg.

– Feel your horse move his haunches to the inside of the circle (to the left), and release your aids to reward him.

You can then choose to stop, and allow your horse to return to his previous path around the circle, or repeat this sequence of aids to keep your horse's haunches in.

Either way, let the horse know you appreciate his efforts with praise.

Progress comes from frequent repetition of essential exercises—as long as they're alternated with periods of rest and relaxation.[78]

Some points to keep in mind when you're performing this exercise:

– Make sure your horse's shoulders stay on the circle. The horse's track shouldn't change in such a way that the shoulders move in and the circle gets smaller (one of the most common mistakes that gets made with this exercise).

– Be careful not to ask for too deep of an angle. "Avoid an exaggerated movement of the haunches (a maximum of 30°–35°) that would kill the movement of the shoulders, which must precede the movement of the hindquarters."[79]

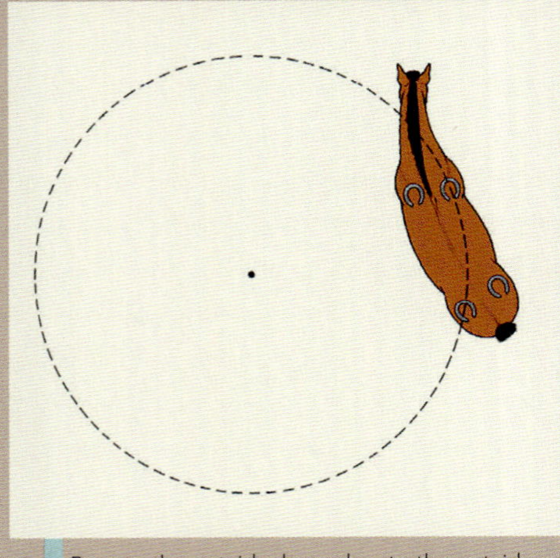

Bent to the outside, haunches to the outside.

3. Bent to the Outside, Haunches to the Outside

On the circle, maintaining bend to the outside, you move the haunches outward for one or several strides.

This exercise, which follows the same logic as the previous one, can be practiced in-hand or under saddle. It encourages the horse to work through his shoulders and use his inside hind leg. It should first be performed on a large circle (which you can gradually reduce to a 6-meter volte), then in half-circles and finally in reverse half-circles. The smaller the circle, the more difficult this exercise becomes.

For this exercise to be executed correctly, the inside hind leg must step under the horse's body and cross in front of the outside hind leg.

Start by asking for this movement on a 16-meter circle around X.[80] This will give you a good reference point—one of the challenges of this exercise is getting the haunches to move to the outside without the shoulders leaving the track of the circle.

Step by Step

Starting from a circle to the left:
– Bring the outside (right) hand out wide to bring the tip of the horse's nose to the outside.
– Shift the inside (left) leg back, applying single-leg pressure to the horse's body.

– Slow the horse down slightly with pressure from the left rein, at the same time as your inside leg is acting.
– Encourage momentum (but not an increase in speed) with that inside leg.
– Feel your horse move his haunches to the outside of the circle (to the right), and release your aids to reward him.

You can then choose to stop, and allow your horse to return to his previous path around the circle, or repeat this sequence of aids to keep your horse's haunches out.

Either way, let the horse know you appreciate his efforts with praise.

Progress comes from frequent repetition of essential exercises—as long as they're alternated with periods of rest and relaxation.

Some points to keep in mind when you're performing this exercise:
– Make sure your horse's shoulders stay on the circle. The horse's track shouldn't change in such a way that the shoulders move in and the circle gets smaller (one of the most common mistakes that gets made with this exercise).[81]
– Be careful not to ask for too deep of an angle. "Avoid an exaggerated movement of the haunches (a maximum of 30°–35°) that would kill the movement of the shoulders, which must precede the movement of the hindquarters."[82]

Common Mistakes with This Exercise

Mistakes by the Rider

– Coordinating the aids poorly, which means the rider can't successfully ask for the right movements from the horse, and also prevents her from dealing with any mistakes made or difficulties encountered by the horse.
– Failing to keep the horse's energy up with the inside leg (the left leg, in our example on a circle to the left).
– Asking for too much bend, or for the haunches to move too far to the outside, either of which will result in the horse losing the correct overall bend throughout his body.

Mistakes by the Horse

– Failing to stay on the track of the original circle, and making it bigger or smaller instead.
– Speeding up or slowing down.
– Losing the correct overall bend in his body, either through too much bend or too much of an angle in his haunches (this means you need to ask him for less).

4. Bent to the Inside, Haunches to the Inside

This exercise is especially interesting because it's performed in the same position as half-pass: the horse is bent with his haunches to the inside. "Begun at a walk [for a few strides], practiced at a trot, mastered at the canter," it allows you to prepare the horse for true collection by encouraging him to lower his hindquarters and take his own weight off his forehand.

The horse is bent, and moves around a circle of your chosen size with his haunches just to the inside of the circle, with the tracks of the forelegs and hind legs fairly close together. Forward movement is valuable, in terms of keeping up the horse's energy and maintaining the regularity of his gait (helping him stay balanced), but it's okay to allow your horse to lose a little bit of momentum (at the walk and trot, at least) when he first begins to try this exercise, in order to let him focus on bending him-

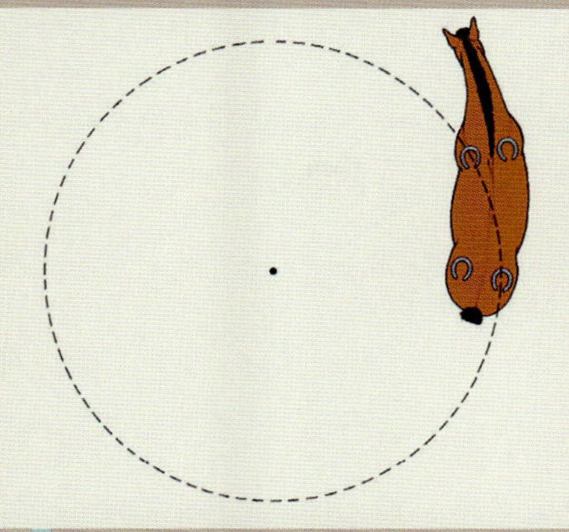

Bent to the inside, haunches to the inside— essentially, moving in renvers on a circle.

self correctly and flexing and engaging his inside hind leg. Worry about his impulsion later! It's better to start a little slow than to demand too much from the start, jostling and nagging a horse who simply doesn't have the strength or flexibility to give you what you're asking for.

As in the first and second exercises ("Bent to the Inside, Haunches to the Outside" and "Bent to the Outside, Haunches to the Inside," pp. 52 and 53), start at a walk, and take your time.

Step by Step

Starting from a circle to the left:
– Bring the tip of the horse's nose to the inside (left).
– While maintaining the horse's overall bend (to the left), shift the outside (right) leg to apply single-leg pressure and move the haunches to the inside, for a few strides.
– Then allow the horse to walk straight for a few strides, and praise him.

Progress comes from frequent repetition— as long as exercises are alternated with periods of rest and relaxation.

To perform the exercise starting from a circle to the right, reverse the aids.

This exercise should be done in a state of calm, gradually, beginning at the walk on a 20-meter circle, and then a 16-meter circle (at

55

X), and then a 10-meter circle. Only make your circle smaller if your horse feels comfortable and flexible beneath you.[83] The same principles apply when you work at a trot or a canter.

The most common mistake with this exercise is losing the horse's bend; as you shift his haunches to the inside, the horse counter-bends and "leans" on your inside leg. To avoid this, keep your inside leg at the girth, and move the horse's haunches very slightly. His energy should always "push" toward his center of gravity. When his haunches move to the inside, his outside hind leg should be tracking in line with his inside foreleg.

If you do all of this correctly but the horse still starts to counter-bend, ask for a forward stride, still bent, with your inside leg only, and this should help straighten him. You can also try pushing him to the outside with your inside leg (as if to enlarge your circle).

As for the other exercises, there are some things to keep in mind:

Common Mistakes with This Exercise

Mistakes by the Rider

– Coordinating the aids poorly, which means the rider can't successfully ask for the right movements from the horse, and also prevents her from dealing with any mistakes made or difficulties encountered by the horse.

Mistakes by the Horse

– Failing to stay on the track of the original circle, and making it bigger or smaller instead.
– Speeding up or slowing down.
– Losing the correct overall bend in his body, either through too much bend or counter-bend, which means he's unbalanced (and you need to work on maintaining balance and straightness; pick a slower gait, and try again).

– Make sure your horse's shoulders stay on the circle. The horse's track shouldn't change in such a way that the shoulders move in and the circle gets smaller (one of the most common mistakes that gets made with this exercise[81]).
– Be careful not to ask for too deep of an angle. "Avoid an exaggerated movement of the haunches (a maximum of 30°–35°) that would kill the movement of the shoulders, which must precede the movement of the hindquarters."[84]

The Reverse Pirouette

A *reverse pirouette*[85] is a complete turn-on-the-forehand (moving the haunches around the shoulders); the *reverse half-pirouette*, which is only a half-turn-on-the-forehand, is naturally an easier starting point for a gradual approach.

If the haunches are moving from left to right, then this is considered a turn around the left shoulder. In this case, as an example:
– The left leg pushes the haunches around.
– The right leg (the leg responsible for the horse's impulsion) prevents the horse from stepping backward.
– The overall position of the horse is angled a bit to the right (very slightly in the direction of the movement).
– Your hands frame the horse's shoulders to prevent him from falling out in either direction.

The left hind leg should cross clearly in front of the right hind leg; the left foreleg should, ideally, rise with each of the horse's steps but come down in the same place. This exercise should be performed with your horse square—without bend in either direction and with his spine as straight as possible.

This exercise should be reserved for a horse that's already relaxed and supple, and should only be practiced at a walk, at first. Take your time; you should feel as though your horse is pivoting calmly, and moving with measured, even steps.

You can work your way toward this exercise by starting with "Bent to the Inside, Haunches

Working toward a successful pirouette at canter.

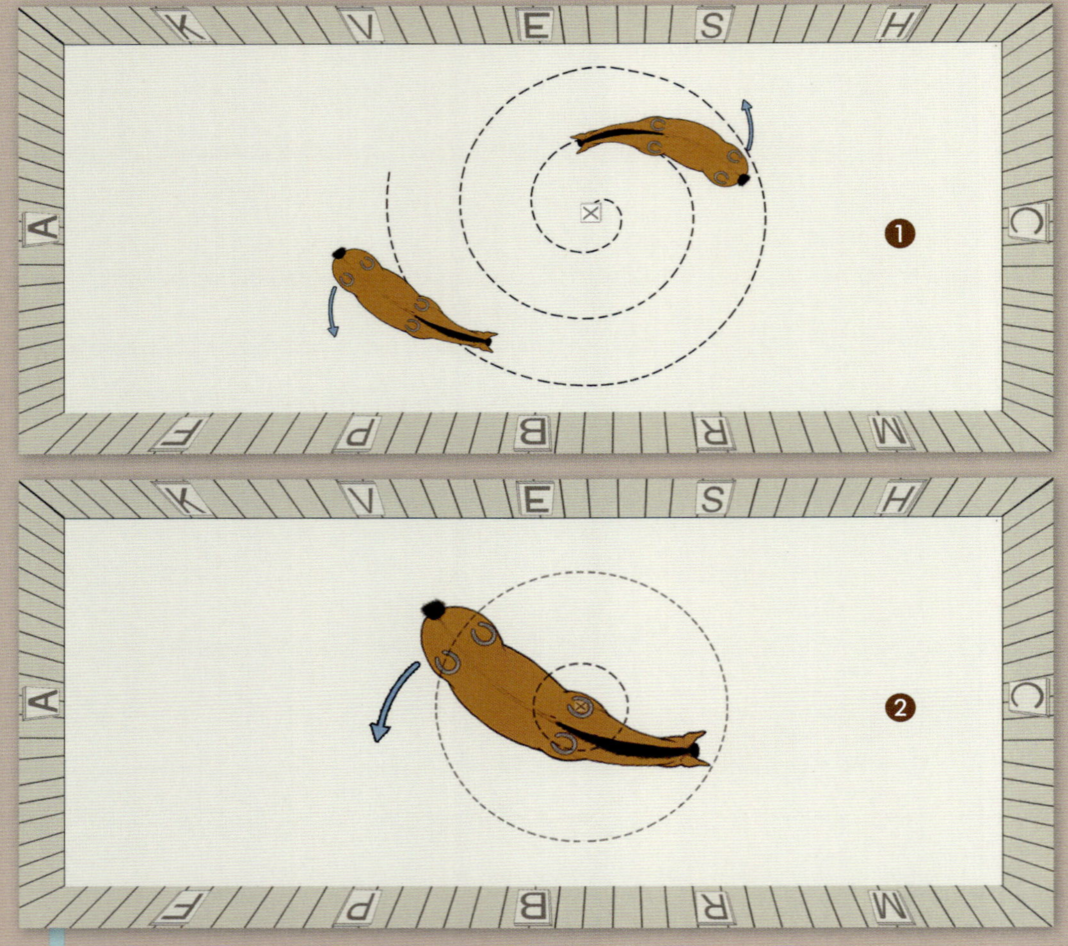

Shift the haunches to the outside and reduce the size of the circle (1), until the horse is doing a half-turn- or a full turn-on-the-forehand (specifically, around the inside shoulder) (2).

The reverse pirouette is a relaxation exercise, meant to stretch and supple your horse—you can't perform it successfully using force. Ideally, you should be able to take a step in reverse pirouette, stop, and then ask for another step, or perform a reverse half-pirouette (or an entire reverse pirouette) without pausing, and do each with equal ease. If you can't stop the movement whenever you want to, then your horse is going too fast, and the exercise isn't having the right effect—either he isn't flexible enough and strong enough to do it correctly yet, or your aids may not be coordinated, positioned, or timed properly (you aren't releasing them with each step before asking for the next step, or you're too abrupt, or you're not using them clearly).

to the Outside (see page 52) and gradually (*very gradually*) decreasing the size of your circle.

How to Approach This Exercise

You shouldn't try to guide your horse into a reverse pirouette without plenty of preparation. Whether your horse is doing it for the first time, or you are, you should work your way toward the reverse pirouette gradually.

1. First, starting from a halt along the wall, ask for a half-turn *around* the forehand, with the horse's front legs moving along a half-circle 4 meters in radius. Once you've given it a try, stop your horse and give him a pat.

2. When the horse is able to do this without difficulty, ask for the same half-turn from a halt along the wall, but this time try to make the forelegs move along a half-circle 1 meter in radius. Once you've given it a try, stop your horse and give him a pat.

3. Finally, repeat the same exercise but ask the shoulders to stay in one place. Once you've given it a try, stop your horse and give him a pat.

When all of the above movements are easy for you and your horse starting from a halt, you can try them starting from a walk (on the inside track of the arena, a few feet from the wall).

1. With your horse at a walk on the track, slow him down and ask for a half-turn *around* the forehand, with the front legs moving along a half-circle 4 meters in radius. Once you've given it a try, without any break in the movement, let your reins lengthen gradually and allow your horse to walk on a long rein, and then give him a pat.

2. With your horse at a walk on the track, slow him down and ask for the same half-turn, but this time try to make the forelegs move along a half-circle 1 meter in radius. Once you've given it a try, without any break in the movement, let your reins lengthen gradually and allow your horse to walk on a long rein, and then give him a pat.

3. With your horse at a walk on the track, slow him down and ask for a half-turn with the shoulders staying in one place. Once you've given it a try, without any break in the movement, let your reins lengthen gradually and allow your horse to walk on a long rein, and then give him a pat.

With each half-turn, change direction.

To perform a successful half-turn at the walk, take care most of all to slow down—to make sure the walk is relaxed and rhythmic before you begin the movement.

You can then try the same sequence of exercises on the centerline, starting on a line parallel to the short side of the arena (first from the halt, then at the walk, reducing the size of the maneuver from 4 meters to 1 meter and then performing half a turn in place).

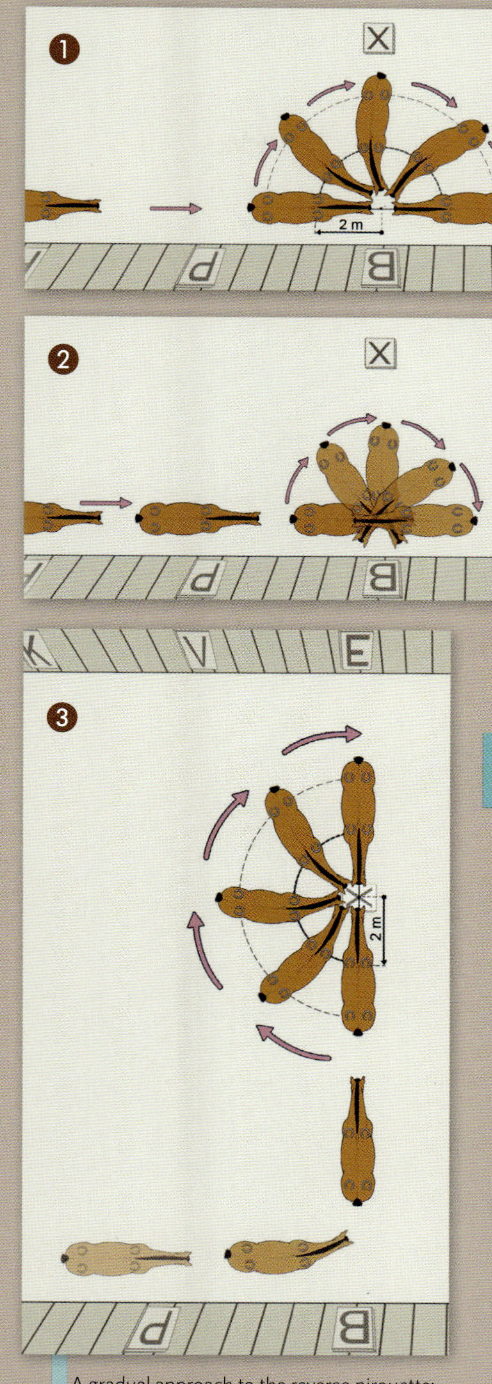

A gradual approach to the reverse pirouette; a half-turn *around* the forehand, along the wall, with the shoulders moving along a 2-meter half-circle (1); a half-turn *on* the forehand, on the inside track a few feet from the wall (2); a half-turn around the forehand (3) and then on the forehand, starting on a line parallel to the short side of the arena, some distance from the wall.

59

Pirouette at the canter.

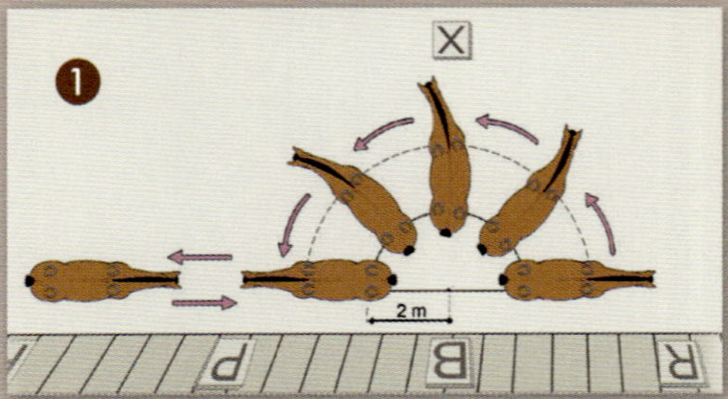

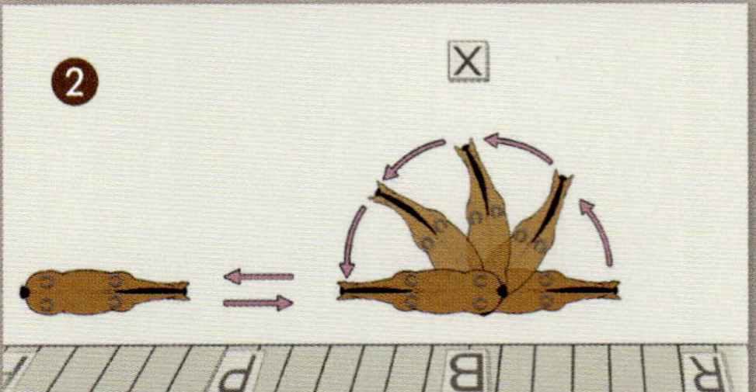

A gradual approach to the pirouette; a half-turn *around* the haunches, with the haunches moving along a 2-meter circle, against the wall (1); a half-turn *on* the haunches, against the wall (2).

This is a great way to develop your own finesse, lightness, and ability to coordinate your aids. Apply yourself and try to communicate with your horse as precisely as possible: if you want his shoulders to move along a 4-meter half-circle, then make sure you're guiding him in a circle, not a 4-meter oval or a misshapen potato. It's very important to successfully complete each variation on the exercise before moving on to a more complicated variation. And don't make the circle the horse is moving along smaller, as you work toward a reverse pirouette, unless your horse feels comfortable and flexible at the circle's current size.

When a reverse pirouette is performed with the forehand remaining in one spot, it's still important for the horse's front legs, as his "pivot," to keep stepping in place. If he doesn't pick up his front feet with energy, then his forelegs are "stuck," which is an issue that needs to be resolved (it may be due to poor coordination of your aids, a lack of impulsion, a horse who's hollow or not on the bit, or another problem).

The Half-Turn on the Haunches

In contrast to the half-turn on the forehand, this movement involves revolving the shoulders around the haunches. The horse can be either straight or bent in the direction of his movement. As with the reverse pirouette, the half-turn here is easier to achieve than the full turn, and you should only try a full turn when you and your horse are both comfortable with the half-turn.

This exercise should be reserved for a horse that is already relaxed, supple, and strong, and should be practiced at the walk. Take your time; you should feel as though your horse is able to pivot in a state of calm, with measured, and even steps.

You can work your way toward this exercise by starting with "Bent to the Outside, Haunches to the Inside" (see page 53) and gradually (*very* gradually) decreasing the size of your circle.

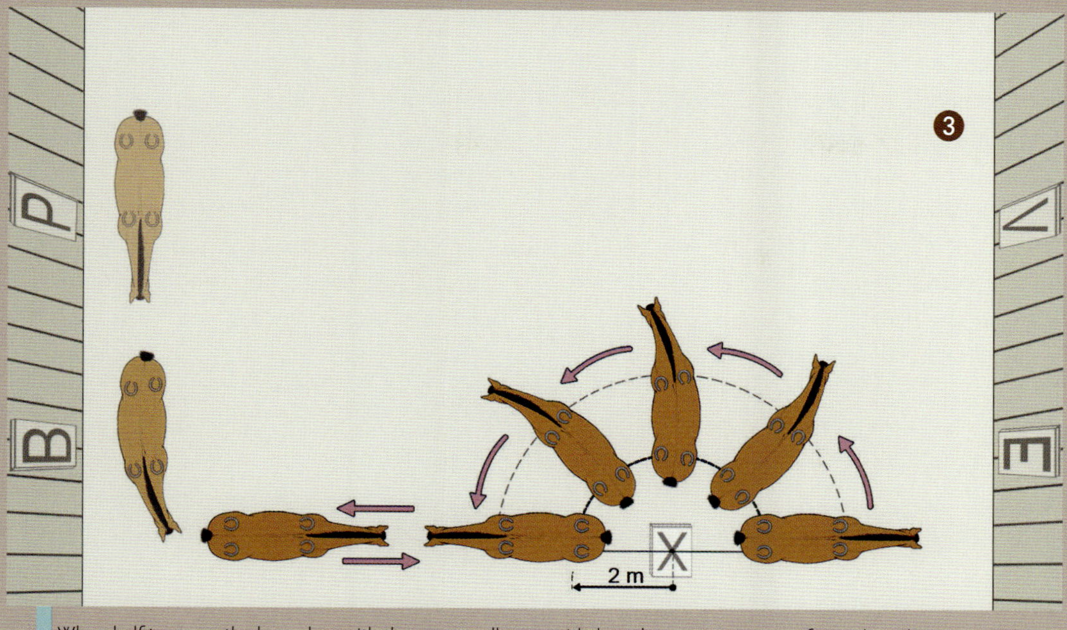

When half-turns on the haunches with the arena wall as a guide have become easy to perform, the rider can move on to half-turns around the haunches (3), then on the haunches, starting on a line parallel to the short side of the arena, some distance from the wall.

Step by Step

If the forehand is moving from left to right, then this is considered a half-turn around the right hind leg. In this case, as an example:

– The rider's left leg holds the haunches still (or at least limits their movement).

– The rider's right leg (the leg responsible for the horse's impulsion) prevents the horse from stepping backward.

– The overall position of the horse is angled a bit to the right (very slightly in the direction of the movement).

– Your hands direct the horse's shoulders to move around his haunches.

The left hind leg should cross clearly in front of the right hind leg, which should, ideally, rise with each of the horse's steps but come down in the same place. The variations of this exercise, and their increasing difficulty, follow the same pattern as for the reverse half-pirouette: start with the horse at a halt, along the wall. At the end of the movement, ask your horse to re-turn to a halt. When you've successfully worked your way through all the variations starting from a halt and returning to a halt, then you can try them at a walk (along the wall), and then let your horse return to a walk.

You shouldn't try to guide your horse into a full turn without plenty of preparation. Whether your horse is doing it for the first time, or you are, you should work your way toward the full turn gradually.

Ideally, you should be able to take a step in a turn-on-the-haunches, stop, and then ask for another step, or perform a half-turn (or a full turn) without pausing, and do each with equal ease. If you can't stop the movement whenever you want to, then your horse is going too fast, and the exercise isn't having the right effect—either he isn't flexible enough and strong enough to do it correctly yet, or your aids may not be coordinated, positioned, or timed properly (you aren't releasing them with each step before asking for the next step, or you're too abrupt, or you're not using them clearly).

1. First, starting from a halt along the wall, ask for a half-turn *around* the haunches, with the horse's hind legs moving along a half-circle 4 meters in radius. Once you've given it a try, stop your horse and give him a pat.

2. When the horse is able to do the above without difficulty, ask for the same half-turn, from a halt along the wall, but this time try to make the haunches move along a half-circle 1 meter in radius. Once you've given it a try, stop your horse and give him a pat.

3. Finally, repeat the same exercise but ask the haunches to stay in one place. Once you've given it a try, stop your horse and give him a pat.

When all of the above movements are easy for you and your horse starting from a halt, you can try them starting from a walk (on the inside track of the arena, a few feet from the wall).

1. With your horse at a walk on the track, slow him down and ask for a half-turn *around* the haunches, with the hind legs moving along a half-circle 4 meters in radius. Once you've given it a try, without any break in the movement, let your reins lengthen gradually and allow your horse to walk on a long rein, and then give him a pat.

2. With your horse at a walk on the track, slow him down and ask for the same half-turn, but this time try to make the haunches move along a half-circle 1 meter in radius. Once you've given it a try, without any break in the movement, let your reins lengthen gradually and allow your horse to walk on a long rein, and then give him a pat.

3. With your horse at a walk on the track, slow him down and ask for a half-turn with the haunches staying in one place. Once you've given it a try, without any break in the movement, let your reins lengthen gradually and allow your horse to walk on a long rein, and then give him a pat.

With each half-turn, change direction.

To perform a successful half-turn at the walk, take care most of all to slow down—to make sure the walk is relaxed and rhythmic before you begin the movement.

Then try the same sequence of exercises on the centerline, starting on a line parallel to the short side of the arena (first from the halt, then at the walk, reducing the size of the maneuver from 4 meters to 1 meter and then performing half a turn in place).

This is a great way to develop your own finesse, lightness, and ability to coordinate your aids. Apply yourself and try to communicate with your horse as precisely as possible: if you want his haunches to move along a 4-meter half-circle, then make sure you're guiding him in a circle, not a 4-meter oval or a misshapen potato. It's very important to successfully complete each variation on the exercise before moving on to a more complicated variation. And don't make the circle the horse is moving along smaller, as you work toward a reverse pirouette, unless your horse feels comfortable and flexible at the circle's current size.

The half-turn-on-the-haunches allows the horse to change his way of holding himself and shift his weight onto his hindquarters, which engages his back and haunches fully, from a biomechanical point of view. This will mean he slows down, at first—don't stop him, but rather give him time to perform one step of

> When a turn on the haunches is performed with the haunches remaining in one spot, it's still important for the horse's hind legs, as his "pivot," to keep stepping in place. If he doesn't pick up his hind feet with energy, then his hind legs are "stuck," which is an issue that needs to be resolved (it may be due to poor coordination of your aids, a lack of impulsion, a horse who's hollow or not on the bit, or another problem).

the half-turn, and then another, and then another. This will allow him to stay calm and to understand the movement he's being asked to perform—and it will let the exercise do its job, suppling, stretching, and relaxing him.

Pirouette at the walk.

Pirouette at a canter.

The Half-Pirouette and the Pirouette

These movements are performed at the walk or the canter; the horse turns on his haunches, while bent in the direction of travel.

These are difficult maneuvers, no matter which gait you're working in, and they're intended for experienced horses who are supple and relaxed. They always require the horse to be moving in collection—they are part of the *haut école*, the "high school" of dressage movements.

You can work your way toward this exercise by starting with "Bent to the Inside, Haunches to the Inside" (see page 55) and gradually (*very* gradually) decreasing the size of your circle. Since your horse will be moving around that circle while bent to the inside, with his haunches to the inside, the horse will be turning *around* his haunches, and then *on* his haunches, as the circle continues to shrink. A half-pirouette will be three or four canter strides; a full pirouette is a complete turn with six to eight canter strides. Both will require flexibility and balance from you and your horse.

The inside hind leg will be taking most and sometimes all of the horse's weight, and will not change position (that is, it'll rise and fall with each of the horse's steps, but it should take off from and come down in the same place each time). The hind legs will not cross each other at all, while the forelegs will cross each other to the greatest degree possible. The horse must balance himself on that inside hind leg, lower his inside hip, and collect himself. His forehand will become lighter, encouraging flexibility and mobility in his shoulders and allowing his forelegs to achieve their full range of motion.

Mistakes in the Half-Pirouette and Pirouette

Mistakes by the Rider

– Coordinating the aids poorly—but that doesn't mean you should stop, since refining the precision of your aids is one of the things this movement will help you do.

Mistakes by the Horse

– "Breaking" in his neck or back, bending too sharply in one area instead of in a smooth curve of his entire body.
– Going off-track or moving sideways.
– Losing rhythm and falling into a disunited canter.
– Leading with his hindquarters, before or after the movement.
– Losing his balance.
– Losing rhythm, regularity, or impulsion in his hindquarters.
– Failing to lower his hips.
– Losing stability, or dropping the contact with the rider's hands.

"Work on two tracks is any exercise in which the horse moves at an angle such that his forehand and hindquarters follow two separate tracks. This work aims to increase the overall mobility of the horse, to soften his loins and the upper joints of his limbs, and to allow the rider to direct the horse's energy."[86]
Manuel d'Équitation,
[Manual of Equitation],
FFE (Fédération Française d'Équitation)

Lateral Relaxation Exercises on Two Tracks

It might seem counterintuitive to exercise a horse at diagonal angles that put him on two tracks, when the goal of dressage overall is to straighten the horse. However, working on two tracks is actually about continuing and refining the bending and mobilization of the shoulders and hindquarters that began with the exercises on the circle. A horse can only be straightened if he's supple and relaxed, on both sides of his body; you need to alternate longitudinal stretching with lateral stretching, if you're going to maintain the horse's impulsion and energy and work on his flexibility and suppleness at the same time. Working on two tracks improves positioning and engagement, while longitudinal exercises encourage lift and propulsion. It's as difficult to make a horse straight, energetic, and forward-moving when you train him with nothing but lateral exercises as it is to make a horse flexible and supple, able to cross his legs when asked, with nothing but longitudinal exercises.

So it's up to you to make sure you switch between these categories of exercises, and plan your work with your horse in a way that maximizes the benefits of each. For example:
– Start with the leg-yield, and use the engagement and "bounce" that results to work on canter departs.

– Start with exercises on the circle, and use the practice directing your horse's use of his back in any other exercise.

– Start with shoulder-in, and use the horse's lengthening to work in extension.

The starting point for any work on two tracks is the circle—firstly, because most exercises done on two tracks use the same aids you use to ask your horse to bend on a circle, and secondly, because the first exercise on two tracks that you should start with is spiraling outward from a circle, using your inside leg.

Spiraling Outward from a Circle

It's only with rational, gentle methods, involving no forceful action, that responsiveness and balance can be achieved with the horse.

Nuno Oliveira

Spiraling outward from a circle involves "pushing" the horse in the middle, so he moves sideways without altering the degree of bend in his body, with his inside legs crossing his outside legs.

To ask for this movement, all you need is a little action with your inside leg (which should remain positioned at the girth).

For this exercise to be effective, the horse must respond to the slightest pressure from your leg (and stay "light" against your leg) and maintain his cadence, finding the sweet spot between balance and impulsion. When you first start working on two tracks, your horse probably isn't going to be "light" against your leg right away, and he's also probably going to struggle with keeping an even rhythm. That's okay—these are exactly the kinds of things this exercise will help you work on. But this also means you'll be facing several issues you need to try to fix, right off the bat.

These problems aren't hard to identify, and some of them fall into one of the following categories:

– Your horse speeds up, without "falling out" through either shoulder. Try to slow him down.

– Your horse slows down, without "falling out" through either shoulder. You need to try to encourage his impulsion, using both of your legs.

– Your horse speeds up and *does* "fall out," typically on his outside shoulder.

- You can try to slow him down and control his outside shoulder using your outside rein.

- You can also try strengthening the action of your inside leg, which encourages the engagement of the inside hind leg and will help him find his balance.[87]

– Your horse's hindquarters are "lagging behind," and he's either speeding up or slowing down to compensate for it.

- If he's speeding up, you should slow him down using the outside rein, and then use your inside leg to position his hips before applying both legs to encourage more impulsion in his hindquarters.

- If he's slowing down, hold yourself with energy, and then use your inside leg to position his hips before applying both legs to encourage more impulsion in his hindquarters.

This exercise (when performed at a walk, too, but especially at a trot) will allow you to focus on:

– Helping your horse understand that he needs to yield to the action of your inside leg throughout his body and let it "push" him (your inside rein, by contrast, shouldn't be doing any "pushing").

– Learning to tell whether your horse is getting a "bounce" of energy from crossing his legs during this exercise (the "bounce" will show up if your

In general, it's hard to correct a movement that starts off badly from the beginning, or deteriorates from one stride to the next. In the case of something like a spiral outward from a circle, instead of scrambling to fix a spiraling movement that isn't working well, it's better to back up and redo the circle you started on, making sure your horse is balanced and moving with the right cadence, and then begin the spiral again from a solid foundation.

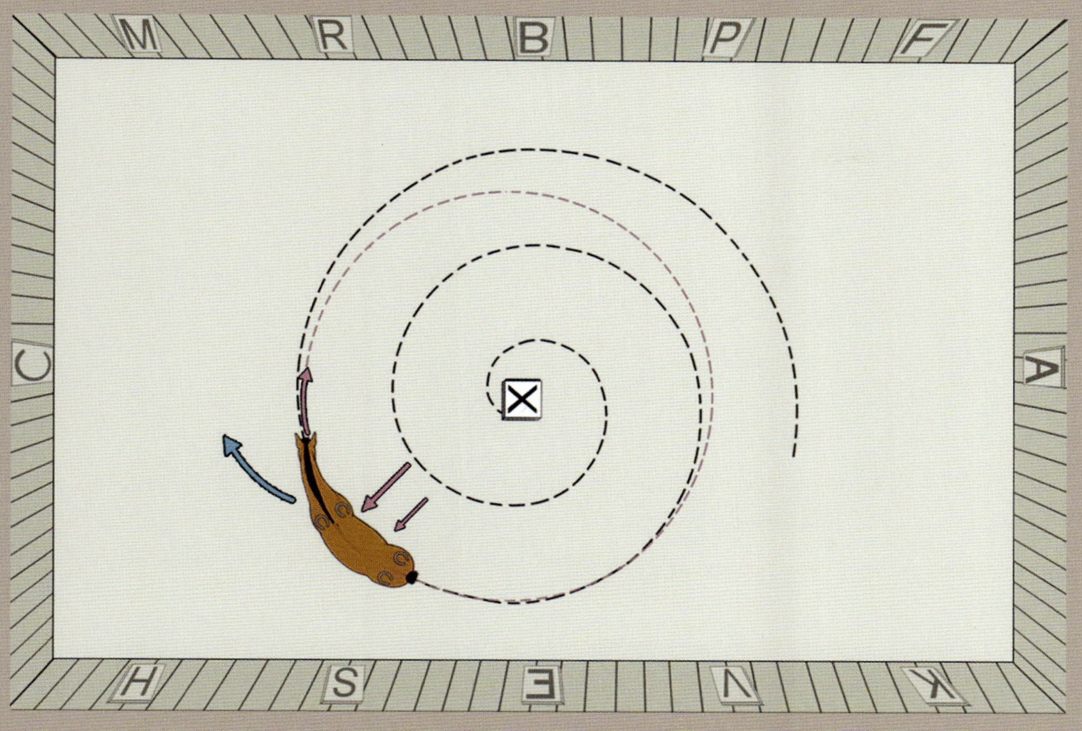

horse is keeping the same cadence and rhythm in his gait and is positioned correctly, so if there's no "bounce," there's an issue with one or more of these things that you should address).

As always, try this movement for only a few strides at first, and then for longer and longer intervals. At more advanced levels, you can even ask the horse to change his stride (to go into extension) during this movement.

The Side-Pass

Don't constantly demand that the horse give the maximum. Know how to wait until he can.

Nuno Oliveira

The term "side-pass" describes a movement in which the horse goes sideways, even if his legs are not crossing each other at first.

The first strides in side-pass are usually achieved as follows, starting in walk:[88]
– Walk along the arena track.

– Two or three strides before the end of the short side, turn.
– You'll then be on an inside track parallel to the long side of the arena, two or three strides from the wall.
– Take advantage of the natural tendency of the young horse to want to return to the wall, out of sheer habit: "push" your horse toward the track with your inside leg.
– He should then take at least a couple steps of side-pass.

Then make the exercise more difficult by turning earlier (farther from the track you're aiming for), and asking for either:
– Maximum movement of the limbs, by rejoining the normal track around the arena as far as possible down the long side.
– A more marked crossing of the horse's legs, if they were only crossing a little or not at all, by rejoining the normal track around the arena as close as possible to the short side.

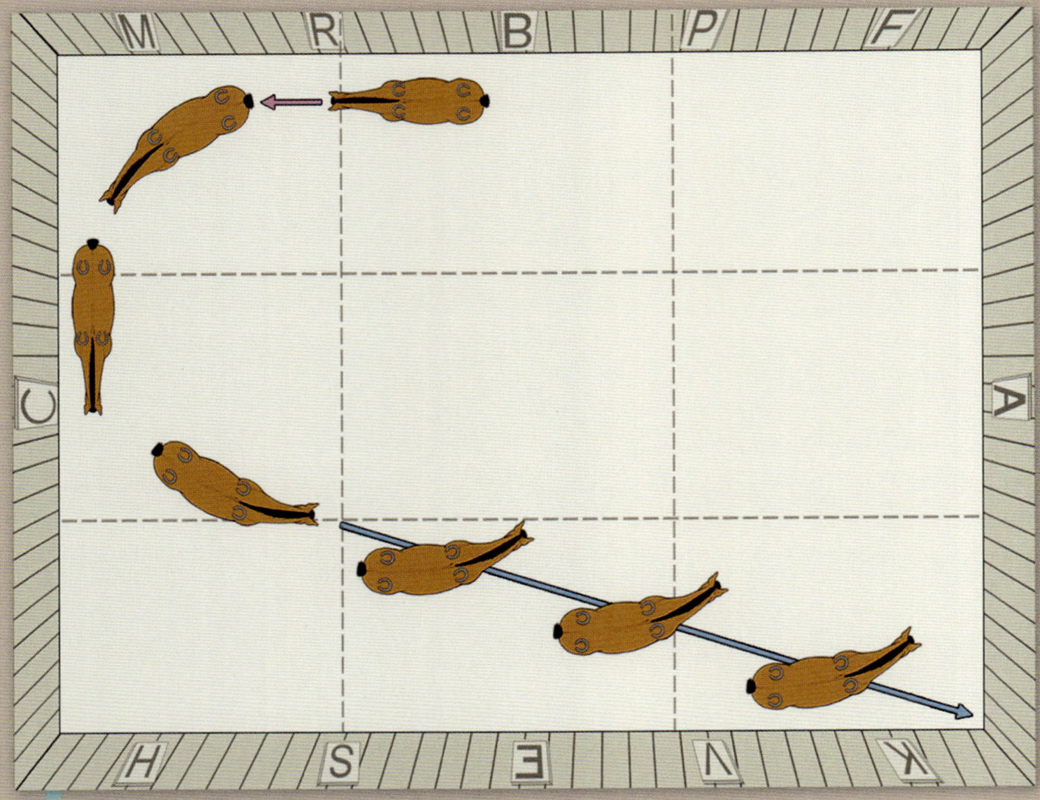

The first steps in side-pass: the key is for the horse to understand that he can get where you're asking him to go by crossing his legs and moving sideways.

Some will consider the horse to be in shoulder-in, at this point, and others will consider him to be leg-yielding;[89] at this stage in his training, though, it doesn't actually matter. The key points here, much like for the spiral outward, are as follows:
– The movement is carried out by the action of your inside leg, not your inside hand or inside rein.
– Your inside leg remains at the girth, and the horse is bending around it, which means he's counter-bending (bending away from the direction of travel).
– Your horse shouldn't be losing rhythm or energy in his gait—this is an especially important point, particularly with a young horse. React to any speeding up or slowing down on his part with a gentle action of your aids, which isn't intended to punish him but rather to help him

understand that he needs to keep his rhythm and energy consistent.
– You should be careful not to have your horse in too active a walk or trot before turning him and taking him into side-pass. Better still, slow him down a little bit right before you begin this exercise, so he takes his time positioning his legs and performs the movement calmly, without tension or any urge to rush.
– Finally, as with any exercise, aim for "lightness" (an "easy," unforced responsiveness to your aids) and a movement that comes readily, without difficulty, at the slightest pressure from your leg.

You can refine this movement further by:
– Straightening it, to take the first step toward a real leg-yield.
– Taking advantage of the horse's bend, to take the first step toward a real shoulder-in.

The Leg-Yield

The challenge of dressage is the mobilization of the horse, gymnastic work that must be done methodically and without haste—because if it isn't done in such a way, you won't get anywhere.

Nuno Oliveira

Definition and Purpose

In the leg-yield, your horse "yields" (hence the name of the exercise) to the action of your leg and walks sideways, crossing his legs, while remaining otherwise straight, from head to tail.

This exercise should have an effect on the horse as a whole, of course, but above all, thanks to the combination of impulsion and the way the horse is crossing his legs as he moves sideways, it should encourage a "bounce" in the gait. Properly executed, the leg-yield encourages both regularity and "bounce" (especially at the trot), while improving the horse's control over and awareness of his legs.

It can be done:
– on the diagonal, with the horse remaining as parallel as possible to the long side of the arena.
– along the wall—in this case, the angle of the horse's body, in relation to the track, shouldn't be more than about 35°.

In this exercise, the sideways movement is just as important as the forward movement. It's essential to maintain impulsion, make sure your horse is crossing his legs, and keep him straight, all at the same time.

Practicing the Leg-Yield

Step by Step

For a left leg-yield (in which, you are asking the horse to yield to your inside leg on his left side, and therefore he is moving to the right (2) on a diagonal):
– After riding through a corner, or turning the horse off the outside track of the arena, make sure your horse is straight.
– Slow his pace to improve balance and give

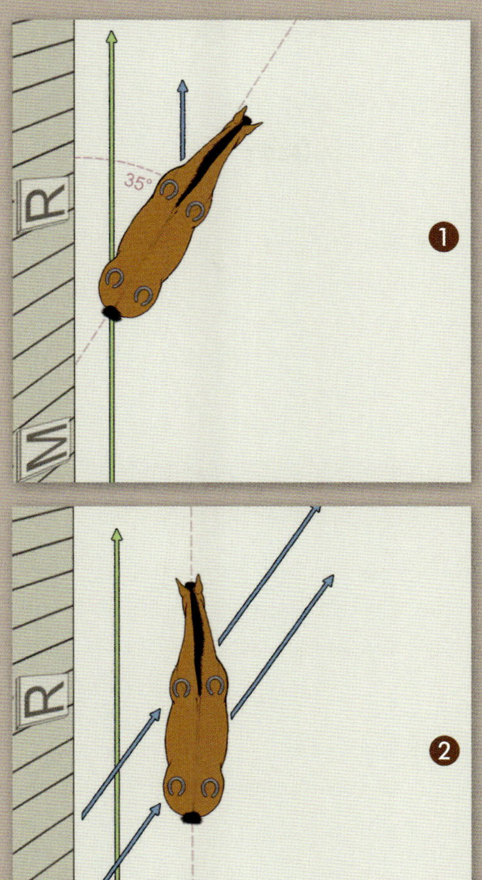

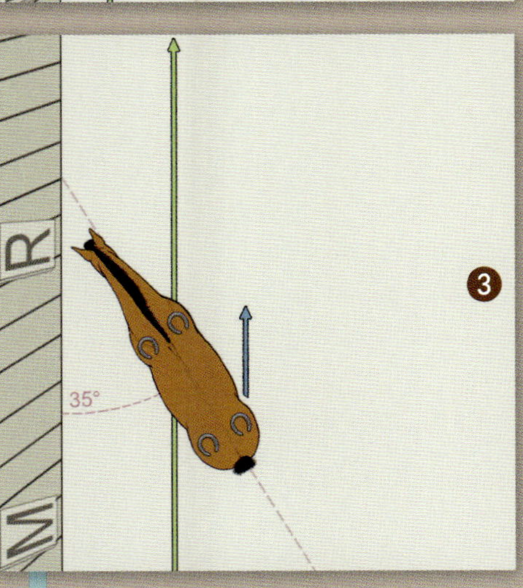

Various approaches to leg-yield along the kickboards (1 and 3) and diagonally away from the kickboards (2). In each case, the horse is straight, with a very slight bend opposite the direction of travel.

71

him time to understand what he's being asked to do.

– Use your inside rein (left) to support the movement.

– Use your outside rein (right) to ask your horse *not* to bend his neck sideways, and to control the movement of his shoulders.

– Use your inside leg (left) to ask him to yield sideways.

– Use your right leg to "receive" him and maintain his forward impulsion.

– Use your weight and your seat as needed: in the direction of travel, if you find you need to encourage your horse's forward or sideways movement, or you need to reinforce the aids of your inside leg; away from the direction of travel, if your horse is rushing; in a neutral, upright, balanced position, if all is going well.

– Look where you're going—this allows you to "point" to the side of the arena you and your horse are moving toward, and it will naturally align your chest and shoulders correctly for the movement.

The horse will be moving sideways, to the right, and remaining straight, with the shoulders slightly preceding the hindquarters, his legs crossing each other with each step, and the cadence of his gait (ideally) unchanged.

In a dressage test, he must maintain a slight bend in his neck, "the rider just able to see the brow bone and the nostril on the side of the bend"[90]; in training, though, it's usually best to seek complete straightness, with no bend in the neck and equal contact on both reins.

You may encounter a variety of problems as you work on the leg-yield:

The leg-yield can be practiced at a walk, a trot, or a canter. Done at a canter, it encourages straightness in the canter overall, and it prepares the horse for changes of lead and improves his straightness during those maneuvers, too[1].

---

1 *Travail au galop et changement de pied* [Work at Canter and Changes of Lead], also by Guillaume Henry

– The hindquarters aren't following the movement properly, and therefore your horse isn't straight. This means you need to slow down your horse's outside shoulder, then reinforce the action of your inside leg to move the hips into the correct position.

– Your horse is rushing and "falling out" through his shoulder. This means you need to straighten him and slow down the shoulder in question.

<table>
<tr><td>

Mistakes in Leg-Yield

Mistakes by the Rider

– Failing to coordinate the aids correctly (this means the horse will lose his straightness).
– Leaning back/letting the upper body "lag behind" the seat.
– Leaning forward/not sitting up straight.
– Emphasizing the action of the inside leg aid too much (this means the horse's hindquarters will outpace his shoulders).
– Lowering the head/looking down, instead of looking in the direction of travel.

Mistakes by the Horse

– Losing his straightness/"breaking" at the base of his neck.
– Outpacing his shoulders with his hindquarters.
– Leading with his shoulders and "dragging" his hindquarters along behind.
– Losing his regularity or his forward energy (crossing his legs too much, without enough forward movement at the same time).
– Rushing in the direction of travel, losing his balance (this means you need to slow down the movement until he's got his balance back, and then resume the exercise—without shifting your body weight in the direction of travel).
– Tilting his head sideways and losing contact on one side (this means you need to straighten his head and get his poll above his mouth again).
– Moving sideways but not forward (this means you need to lessen the angle of the leg-yield and encourage him to go a little more forward).
– Moving forward but not sideways (this means you need to emphasize your inside leg aid, and shift your body weight in the direction you want him to go).

</td></tr>
</table>

Left leg-yield (which is to say, a yielding on the left, with the horse moving to the right.).

– Your horse isn't moving forward with energy. This means you need to keep the rest of your aids in place and emphasize your outside leg aid, to ask him for more impulsion.

– Your horse is slowing down and his hindquarters are outpacing his shoulders. This means either:

- You're "leaving the shoulders behind," and you need to encourage them to move sideways with just as much energy as the hindquarters.

- You're using your inside leg a little too much, and you need to ease off.

You can use the leg-yield to remind your horse, in the course of his training, to pay attention to your inside leg as you transition to canter from the walk:

– Perform a right leg-yield at the walk.

– Shift your right leg forward to the girth (without losing contact with the horse's side).

– Apply pressure at the girth and ask the horse for a canter depart on the right lead.

– After a few canter strides, return to a walk.

– Give the horse praise, and then repeat.

To do the same exercise on the left, reverse the aids.

The Shoulder-In

In shoulder-in, it's the hindquarters that should push, rather than trail behind the horse's neck.

The shoulder-in is riding through a corner, extended along the long side.

If the shoulder-in is executed well, the horse should reach the end of the long side feeling more supple and more relaxed. If the movement's forced, then he'll get there feeling stiffer.

Nuno Oliveira

Definition and Purpose

Shoulder-in is an exercise on two tracks, with the forehand and the hindquarters potentially on two separate tracks apiece. The forelegs cross on an inside track; the hindquarters remain on the outside track, and don't cross. The horse should

Left shoulder-in, at the trot.

be slightly bent around the inside leg, with even bend throughout his body, opposite the direction of travel. "The sum of all the gymnastic movements that can be asked of the horse,"[91] the shoulder-in is sometimes described as "the first and last lesson to give him."[92]

Shoulder-in has many benefits; it makes the horse more flexible throughout his body, frees the shoulders, improves his balance (by encouraging him to step under himself with his hindquarters), and enhances his ability to bend through his back around the rider's inside leg. It also straightens those horses who otherwise have a tendency to bend on straight lines in an effort to escape the rider's aids, increases the suppleness and engagement of the hindquarters, and helps prepare the horse to ride through corners and perform pirouettes and half-pass.

Étienne Saurel, in his *Manuel d'équitation et de dressage* [Equitation and Dressage Manual], very clearly describes the goals of working in shoulder-in: "This lesson [...] brings about:
– Freedom in the shoulders, responsiveness to the hand, and, consequently, lightness in the forehand.
– Suppleness in the hindquarters, responsiveness to the leg, and, consequently, the engagement of the hindquarters.
– Alignment in the spine, which creates harmony between the forehand and the hindquarters.
– Specifically, it encourages freedom in the shoulders because when the horse works with energy, bent in shoulder-in, the right foreleg must engage through its full range of motion, rotating and rising to pass in front of the left foreleg.
– It improves flexibility in the hindquarters because the right hind leg, by contrast, must bend to allow it to step further under the horse than the left hind leg, which also increases the engagement of the hindquarters.
– It increases suppleness and alignment in the spine, because of the flexing and bending required through the back, which must engage through its full range of motion.

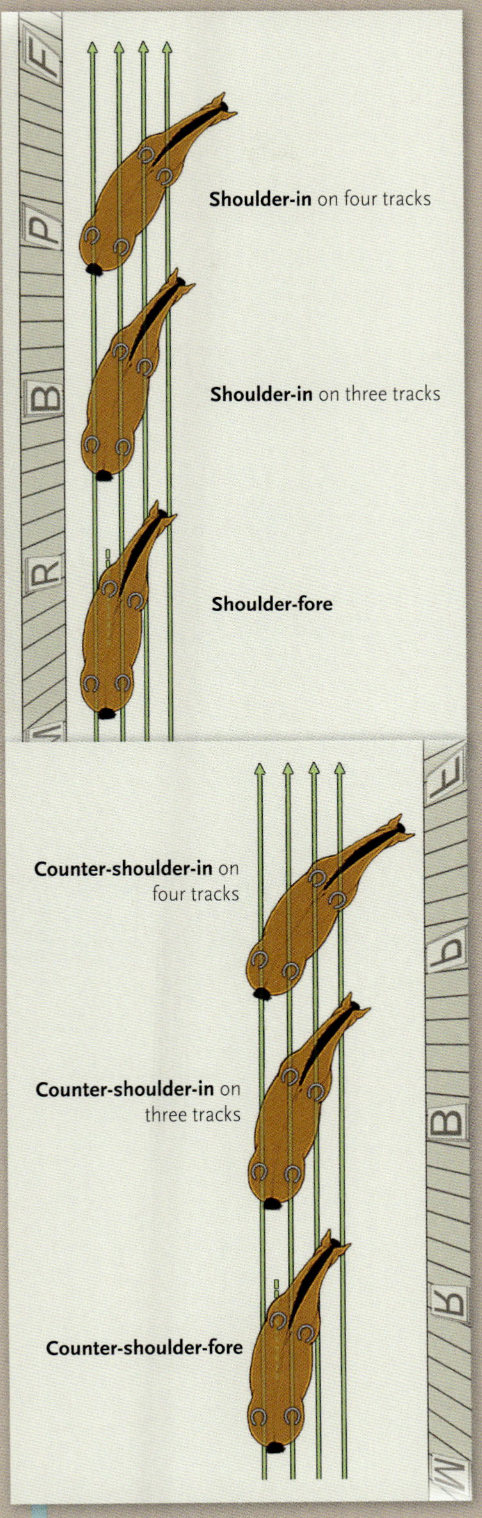

Variations on shoulder-in and counter-shoulder-in.

– It encourages the horse's responsiveness to the hand, because the leg, acting in the same direction as the hand, asks the horse to accept the tension of the rein.

– And it encourages the horse's responsiveness to the leg, because the rein, acting in the same direction as the leg, asks the horse to understand and accept the leg's action."

Shoulder-Fore, Shoulder-In, and Counter-Shoulder-In

There are different "categories" of shoulder-in, depending on the angle of the horse in relation to the direction of travel, and, therefore, the relative position of his shoulders:

– Shoulder-fore.

– Shoulder-in on three tracks.

– Shoulder-in on four tracks.

You may encounter similar problems (with equally similar solutions) when you're spiraling outward from a circle and when you're practicing shoulder-in, but these movements differ in two major ways:

– On a spiral, the hind legs cross along with the forelegs, but in shoulder-in, they don't, which changes the horse's balance in each case: on a spiral, the horse's balance remains level on the horizontal, but in shoulder-in, it rises, closer to a state of collection. The gait "bounces" on a spiral, but it starts to become truly collected in shoulder-in.

– The angle of the bend in the horse is greater in shoulder-in.

Because of these differences, spiraling outward from a circle is a little easier for you and your horse, and it makes great preparation for the shoulder-in precisely because it's the same overall type of movement and you'll encounter some of the same challenges.

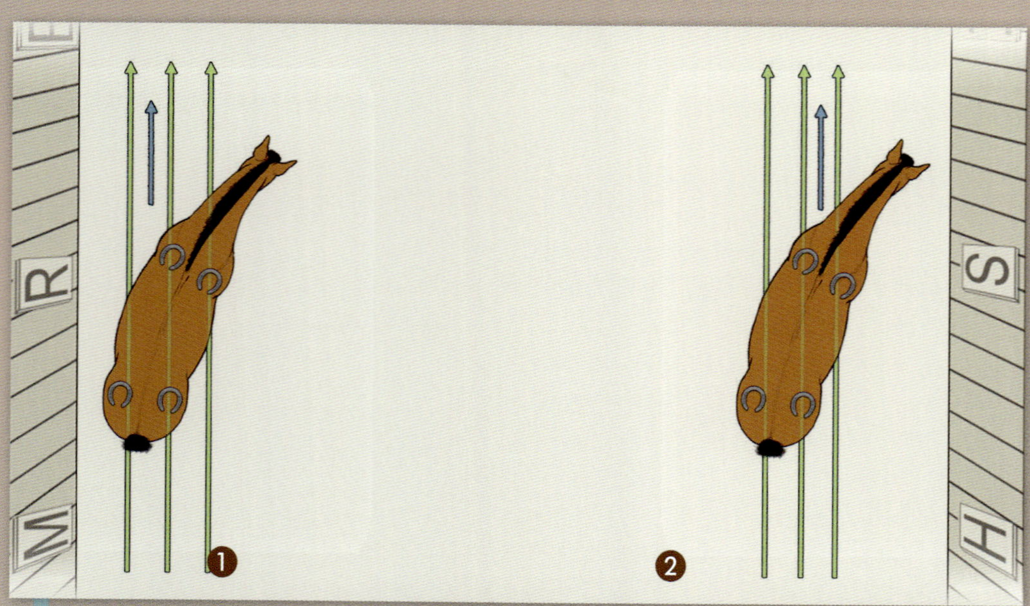

There are no differences, on a fundamental level, between shoulder-in and counter-shoulder-in; the only distinction is the position of the horse relative to the arena kickboards.

But in the first case (1), the horse will have a tendency to want to move toward the middle of the arena (and not bend around the inside leg), while in the second (2), it's the hindquarters that will tend to "fall" toward the inside of the arena.

Each of these movements has its advantages and disadvantages, because of these tendencies, and the rider needs to know how to use those advantages and disadvantages, with her horse's individual skills and faults in mind.

The more extended the position of the shoulders is, the more difficult the exercise is, and the more experienced and relaxed the horse needs to be in order to perform it well.

The position of the shoulders, therefore, depends on the degree of suppleness and relaxation your horse has achieved. Ideally, the angle between the horse's body and the direction of travel should be less than 30 degrees, to maintain the engagement of the inner hind leg and the regularity of the horse's gait. The major mistake made by overeager riders is moving the shoulders too far sideways, trying to maximize the horse's bend; however, what this actually does is cause the hindquarters to "fall out," or even to start crossing the same way the forelegs are crossing, which means the horse is no longer in shoulder-in at all.

When shoulder-in is performed facing the wall instead of facing the center of the arena, it's called counter-shoulder-in.

Practicing Shoulder-In

Step by Step

For a right shoulder-in (with the track on your right, that is):

- Start with the horse on a circle, at walk or trot, with a rhythmic, regular gait and bending aids applied.
- When he completes one circle, as his shoulders leave the track to begin the next circle, push him "through the middle" with your inside (right) leg, bending him but also asking him to move his whole body, so that he starts to go to the left.
- Shift your body weight in the direction of travel.
- Move your outside (left) leg back, so you control the movement of the hindquarters and can hold them in place to keep them from "falling out," along with encouraging impulsion in the outside (left) hind leg.
- Adjust your horse's speed, the movement of

his shoulders, and the position of his forehand with your outside (left) hand.
- Move the inside (right) rein away from the horse's neck, and release it at any time—it also helps control the position of the forehand and the angle of the shoulder-in.
- Apply your aids and then release them, in rhythm with the horse's gait, to create a smooth, continuous movement in shoulder-in. Remember, keeping the aids applied continuously only leads to resistance and tension in the horse; applying the aids and then releasing them, and then applying them again, is what creates a continuous, ongoing movement.

As with any movement, pay attention to the cadence, and act with your outside hand to ask the horse to slow down, or with your inside leg to ask the horse to keep up his momentum.

In general, you should feel like you're "pushing your horse through the middle and toward his outside shoulder."

Your horse then maintains his bend to the right, and moves to the left in counter-bend, with his forelegs crossing and his hind legs not crossing.

In a dressage test, the number of tracks the horse is on doesn't decide the final score for the movement. You should focus on achieving a slight but regular bend throughout the horse's body, and maintaining his balance and the rhythm of his gait.

The essential points required to earn a good score for shoulder-in:

- Maintaining even bend throughout the horse's body, "from head to tail."

- Bending the horse around the inside leg throughout the movement.

- Keeping the walk or trot rhythmic and regular.

- Keeping the horse on the track (rather than allowing him to start moving toward the inside or outside of the arena).

- Keeping the horse's hindquarters positioned correctly (rather than allowing them to "fall out").

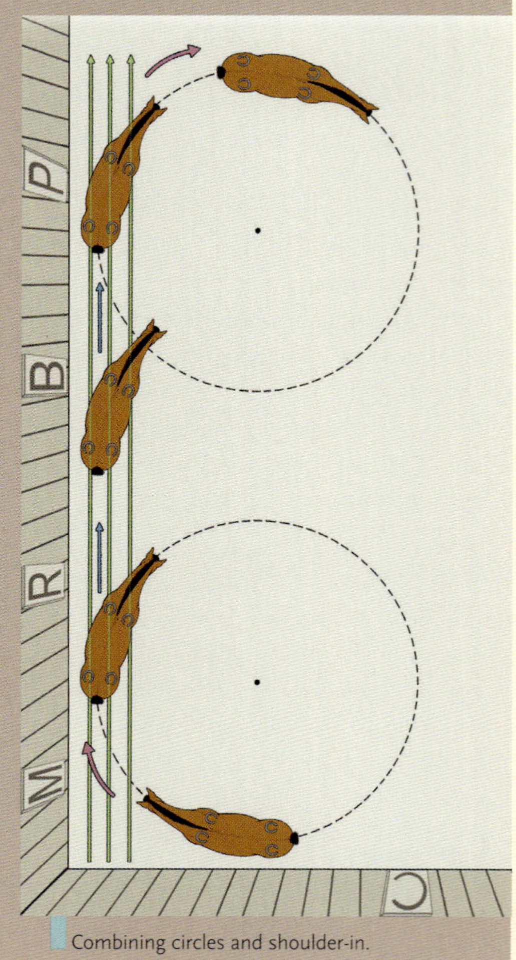

Combining circles and shoulder-in.

a diagonal, or on a circle. Remember, it's not the exercise that makes the difference, but the way the exercise is done; going back and forth across the arena in shoulder-in, at the trot, is useless if the horse is getting heavier, leaning on your hands, falling in or out, or tensing up through the lateral movements. "If the shoulder-in is executed well," writes Nuno Oliveira, "the horse should reach the end of the long side feeling more supple and more relaxed. If the movement's forced, then he'll get there feeling stiffer."

FEI rules state that shoulder-in "is not only an exercise in limbering up, but also in collecting; indeed, the horse at each step must engage his inside hind leg under his body and in front of his outside hind leg, a movement which he cannot execute without lowering the corresponding hip." This means you should be able to feel your horse shifting his weight to his hindquarters. In fact, you should also feel his forehand lighten, and he should slow down a little (because his balance has changed). Ease up on your aids, without changing their position, to encourage him to carry himself; after a few strides like this, return to a circle and allow him to extend his neck as a reward.

You can prepare for shoulder-in on a circle, and end with another circle—this allows you to re-establish the correct bend (if necessary) and prepare for another shoulder-in, if you want to ride these movements in a repeating combination. Or you can allow your horse to lengthen his neck—which relaxes and eases the pressure on his back—and start moving in extension instead.

From the first circle to the last, the horse should retain the rhythm of his gait, his flexibility, and his ease of movement. As with any relaxation exercise, it's frequent repetition, alternated with periods of rest for the horse, that creates progress.

When your horse is flexible, supple, and relaxed, you can ask him for shoulder-in without starting with a circle—on the track, on the centerline, on

Shoulder-fore should be done at canter in the warm-up and cool-down phases. You shouldn't practice this movement until your horse is able to engage his inside hind leg and support his forehand[93] because he'll inevitably keep his croup high; even if he brings his head to the inside, he'll throw his shoulders to the outside. You have to strengthen the canter first, and straighten it using exercises other than shoulder-in.

The presence of the wall at the hindquarters can help the horse keep his hips in the right place.

With a horse who's a little hot, or simply for the sake of variety, you might prefer to work in counter-shoulder-in. Your horse will then have his head toward the wall (which will naturally limit his forward movement) and his hindquarters toward the inside of the arena (which makes it your responsibility to position your legs correctly and control the positioning of his hips so they don't "fall out").

"The exercise is at its most effective when the horse's bend positions his center of gravity directly in front of the thrust coming from the inner hind leg, which is providing the bulk of his propulsion."
Philippe Karl

Mistakes in Shoulder-In

Mistakes by the Rider

– Moving the inside leg too far back, which makes correct bending impossible for the horse.
– Losing contact on the outside leg, or positioning it incorrectly, which makes it difficult or impossible to control the position of the hindquarters.
– Keeping the inside rein too short, which is going to draw the horse into too great a bend and push his outside shoulder to "fall out."
– Looking at the horse's head instead of looking in the direction of travel.

Mistakes by the Horse

– Bending his neck too much (this means you need to adjust his neck position with the reins).
– Bending his body too little (this means you need to review the placement of your aids, or work on the horse's overall roundness with some circles).
– Letting his outside hind foot land on the wrong track, or letting his hindquarters "fall out" entirely (this means you need to double-check the degree of angle you asked him for, slow him down a little, or reposition your outside leg).
– Losing his rhythm (this means you need to reduce the degree of angle you're asking him for, and bring his shoulders a little more in front of his hips).
– Rushing, or speeding up his cadence (this means you need to slow down his outside shoulder, ask him for less movement, or, potentially, return to the circle before asking for shoulder-in again).
– Slowing down (this means you need to double-check the degree of angle you asked him for, or use your seat to ask him to increase the activity of his hindquarters).

Shoulder-fore, in the trot.

The Half-Pass

Definition and Purpose

In the half-pass, the horse travels on "two
tracks," crossing both sets of limbs. He bends
slightly around the rider's inside leg, and stays
as parallel to the long sides of the arena as possible. Nevertheless, the head, neck, and shoulders do precede the hindquarters, if only slightly. The horse should be bent evenly throughout
his body and is bent in the direction of travel.
His legs will cross each other, with both of his
outside legs passing in front of and across
both of his inside legs. The horse's head is
facing the direction of travel, and throughout
this movement, he should be able to maintain
the same cadence and balance in his gait. "The
horse must cross his legs while moving, his
body always remaining parallel to itself."[94] The
purpose of the half-pass is to assess the flexibility of the horse and engage all his suppleness harmoniously.

To train the horse to half-pass you use:

– **Travers**, with the head to the wall; in this variation, the horse, bent in the direction of travel,
is moving with his head toward the wall, with
the difference between his direction of travel
and the track reaching 30 degrees at most.

– **Renvers**, with the croup to the wall; in this variation, the horse, bent in the direction of travel, is
moving with his croup toward the wall, with the
difference between his direction of travel and the
track reaching 30 degrees at most.

Travers (Haunches-In) and Renvers (Haunches-Out)

You should only attempt the half-pass when the
horse is comfortable with both shoulder-in and
haunches-in and is able to move in both positions with ease.[95]

Travers

Ride a circle, bending your horse evenly and
harmoniously through his body. When his forehand reaches the track, lead him into travers
by "containing" him with your outside aids.
He then moves, still bent, with his forehand
on the arena track and his hindquarters on an
inside track. As in the shoulder-in, the distance
between the track the hindquarters are on and
the track the forehand is on should be small, to
start with. It's best to follow the same progression as for shoulder-in, and aim for:

– First, "haunches-fore"...

– ...and then, haunches-in on three tracks...

– ...and finally, haunches-in on four tracks.

To end the movement, let your horse "slide"
down the "corridor" of your aids and return to
a circle.

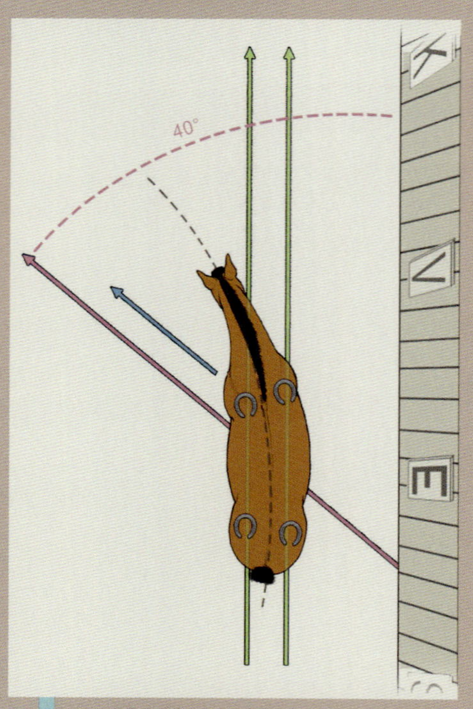

The half-pass.

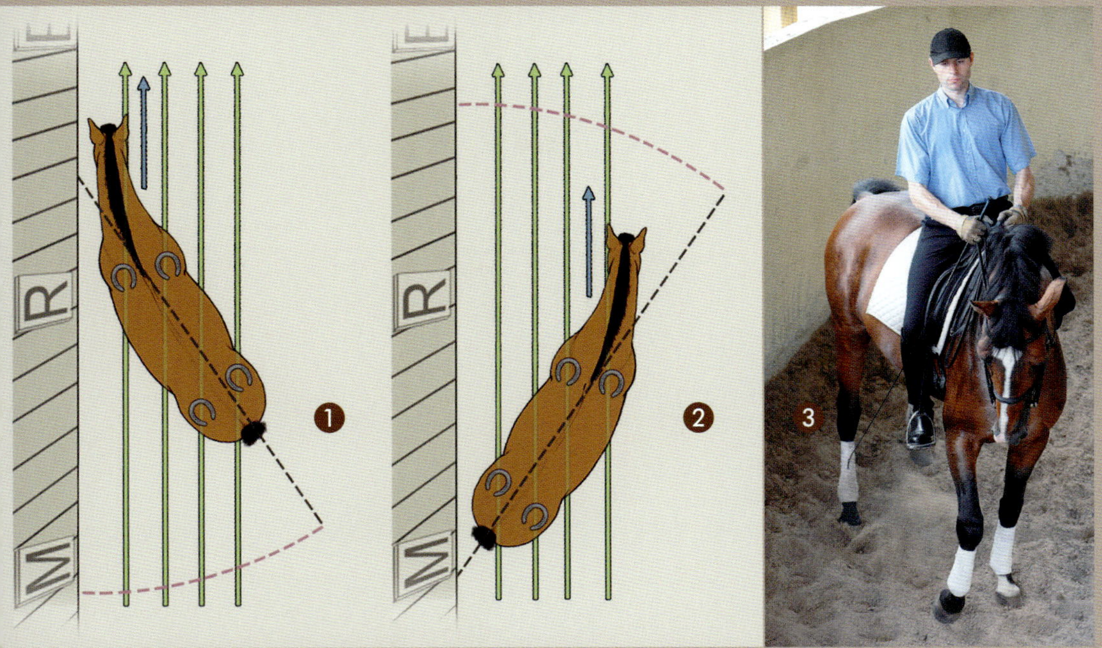

Travers (1), with the head to the wall. Renvers (2 and 3), with the croup to the wall.

Advantages of Travers

"The outside hind leg loses its tendency to avoid its track and develops its ability to line up and reach under the horse's body, to the limit where the inside hind leg is positioned. This pressures the inside hind to step more under the body."[96]

Also, because the horse is facing the wall, his movement is constrained by his awareness of its presence, and you won't need to use your hands as much to keep his forehand in the right position or to maintain the contact and keep him on the bit.

You'll find that combinations of these exercises—shoulder-in, the circle, and haunches-in—are useful and effective; "balanced in this way, by alternating between shoulder-in and haunches-in, with a circle in between,[97] the horse gradually gets better at:
– Arranging his shoulders at an angle relative to his hips, and vice versa.
– Moving his shoulders sideways, relative to his limbs, and bringing his hind legs back into a position of engagement, with his forelegs maintaining a straight position."[98]

Disadvantages of Travers

Working along the arena wall like this can give the horse a bad habit (which then needs to be addressed separately) of following the wall without paying all that much attention to your positioning aids. "The horse is all too inclined to let himself be guided by the wall, instead of responding exclusively to the aids," writes James Fillis, a British-born French horseman and riding master. He was especially specific about this unfortunate side effect: "[The horse] even uses [the wall] as a kind of mental and emotional support, and his natural tendency is always to let the hindquarters drift away and bring the shoulders closer to the wall—hence the difficulty of keeping him straight and really 'containing' him with the rider's legs."[99]
– This proximity to the wall can also create a mental obstacle for the horse, dulling the impulsion, regularity, and cadence of his gait.
– Too great an angle, or a fear of colliding with the wall, can prompt the horse to cross his outside legs not in front of his inside legs,

Example of an exercise where the horse moves into travers, following a circle.

Example of an exercise where the horse moves into a circle, following movement in travers.

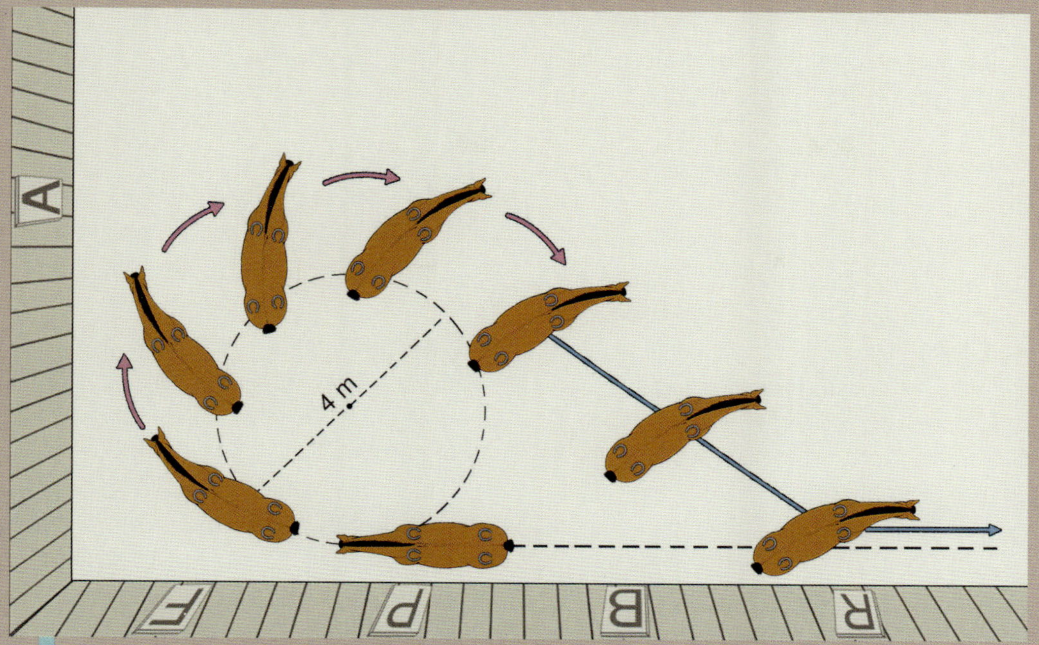

Example of an exercise where the horse moves into renvers, following a half-circle in haunches-in.

but rather behind them, which makes him lose his roundness and his contact with the rider's hand.

Renvers

Renvers isn't often discussed by the authors of classic works on horsemanship. In fact, it usually comes up only in the context of the exercise "Bent to the Outside, Haunches to the Outside" (see page 54).

Start working on renvers along the wall, either at the end of the circle or by turning, along the short side, onto the quarterline. In the latter case, turn, then straighten the horse onto the quarterline, then position your aids as if you wanted to half-pass over to the outside track of the arena. Then "push" the hindquarters onto the track, while keeping the horse moving on two tracks, in order to position the horse in renvers.

As for all the rest of these movements, start with a relatively mild angle.

The advantage of renvers is that it really helps increase the engagement and flexibility of the hindquarters—provided that it's executed with lightness. Your horse has to respond to your inside leg readily, and you should have the feeling that his hindquarters are moving easily.

Renvers lets you ensure that the horse has achieved the degree of flexibility and bend he's going to need for half-pass. In point of fact, the main issue horses and riders run into, with renvers, is that when the hindquarters are moved to the outside of the circle, the horse sometimes ends up counter-bent—because he isn't ready, isn't relaxed, and isn't flexible enough yet for the half-pass. You'll need to combine renvers and shoulder-in, returning to the inside of the arena and following the same principle as for half-pass, which is described next.

Half-Pass

Half-pass should be asked for at first on a relatively gentle angle, and for only a few strides at a time.

Perform shoulder-in, then move onto a diagonal over a few strides:

– If your horse stays bent around your inside leg, take two or three strides in half-pass, then "push" him onto a straight line again, using your inside leg, towards the shoulder in front.

– If your horse loses his bend, "push" him immediately (but without anger: he's learning!) forwards and toward his inside shoulder; you should then go back to working on haunches-in for a while.

If the horse keeps losing his bend, another approach is to "push" him back toward his inside shoulder at an angle before "containing" him again with your outside aids to guide him into half-pass. "Swinging" from one to the other will let you achieve strides in half-pass with the horse balancing correctly.[100]

Step by Step

For a right half-pass on the diagonal:

– Traditionally, you should prepare for half-pass starting from shoulder-in on three tracks; this puts the horse in the correct position (slightly bent) and avoids the hindquarters outpacing the forehand[101] at the start.

– So, begin in right shoulder-in, and turn your shoulders and your gaze in the direction of travel for the half-pass (to the right, toward the end of the diagonal).

– Shift your body weight to the right side of your seat, direct your horse's shoulders with both of your hands, and position the hindquarters with your outside (left) leg.

– Keep your inside (right) leg at the girth, to encourage the horse to maintain his momentum.

– Keep your inside (right) hand low, to encourage the horse to maintain his bend.

– "Contain" the horse within the "corridor" of your outside aids.

– As with the shoulder-in, apply your aids, release them, and then apply them again, in rhythm with your horse's gait, to create continuous movement in a regular cadence and the correct positioning.

– Come out of half-pass with a half-circle to the right, or a return to right shoulder-in.

Finally, don't try to half-pass at an angle of more than about 25 degrees too quickly. This is a classic mistake, which at best makes

It's through "swinging" from half-pass to shoulder-in, and then back to half-pass, that you'll gradually improve the half-pass. Above all, don't keep the horse moving in a flawed half-pass. If you lose control of the half-pass, "push" your horse into shoulder-in, make sure it's correct, and then ask for half-pass again. Remember, a movement that starts badly can't be undone.

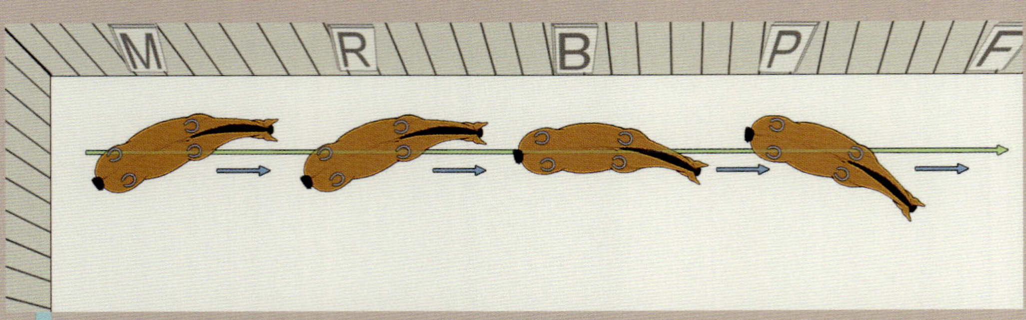

When these movements are easy, the rider can combine them: here, travers followed by shoulder-in.

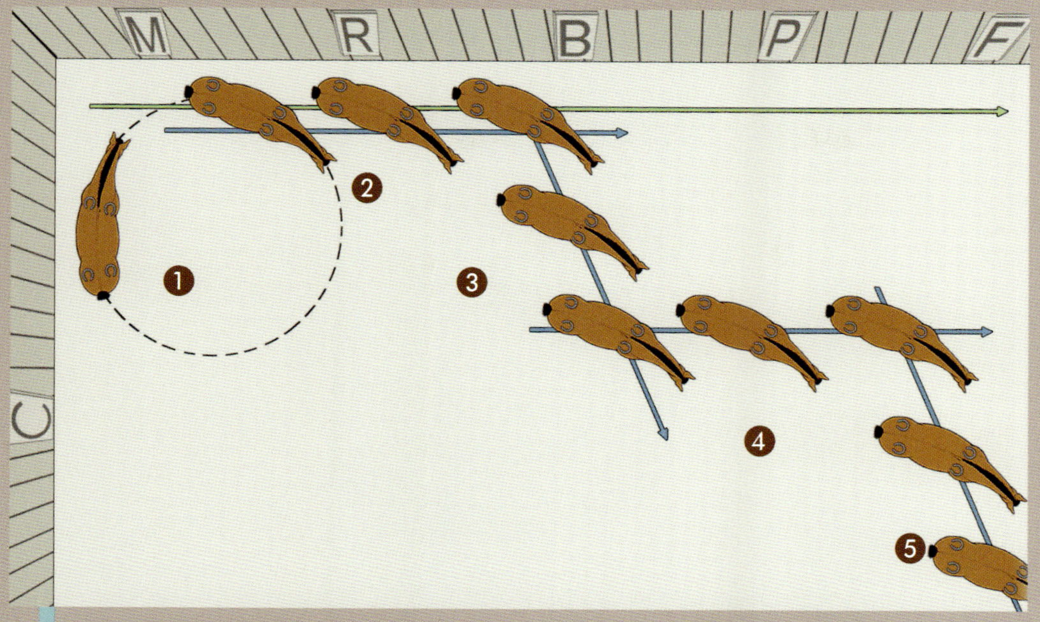

An example of another combination of exercises: a circle (1), followed by shoulder-in (2), and then half-pass (3), back to shoulder-in (4), back to half-pass (5).

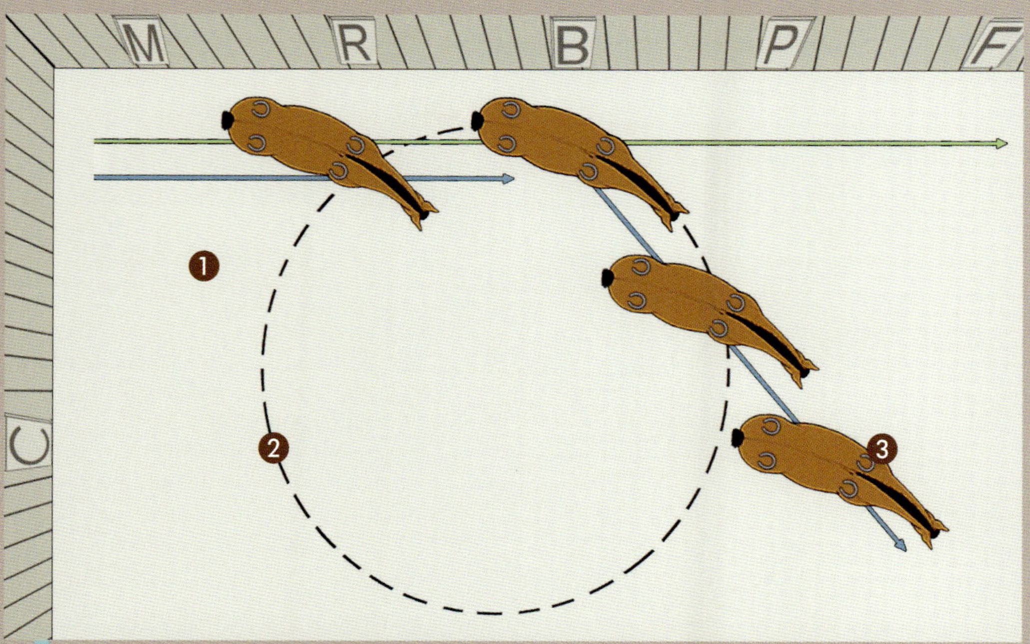

Another example of a possible combination of exercises: shoulder-in (1), followed by a circle (2), followed by half-pass (3). You can vary these kinds of sequences endlessly.

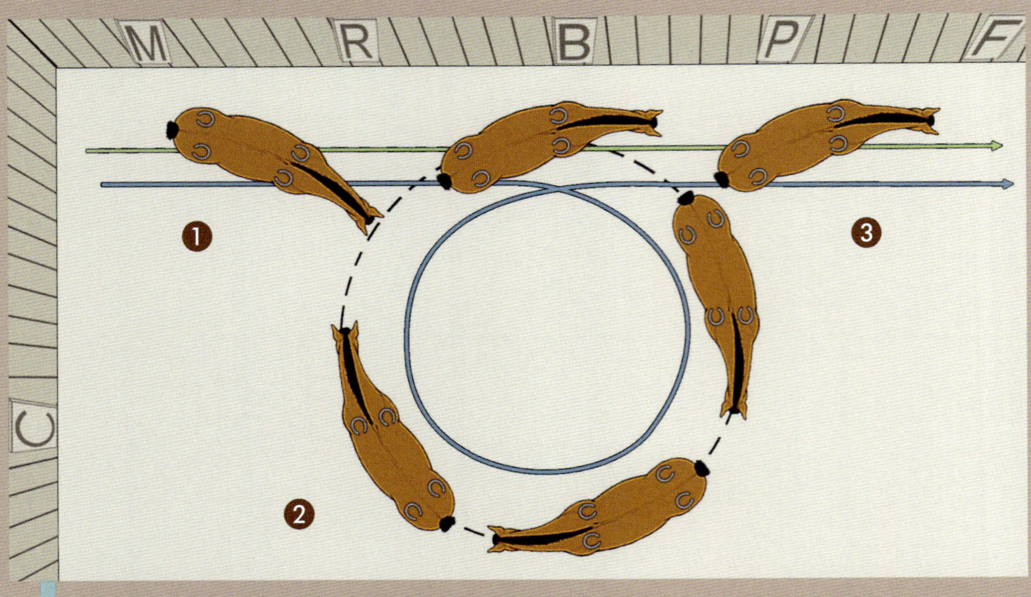

Another example of a possible combination of exercises: shoulder-in (1), followed by a circle (2), followed by travers (3)

the exercise useless, and at worst makes it actively harmful. Also, don't ask the horse to perform half-pass for too long, even at a very shallow angle. The duration of the half-pass (the number of strides you ask the horse to do) should increase very gradually, and only when the horse is comfortable. He should be able to perform the number of strides you ask him for with ease, and be able to move from half-pass to a circle or shoulder-fore and then back to half-pass (a few strides is enough!) without changing his speed or the rhythm of his gait, even extending his gait slightly if you ask him to, and overall staying correctly bent and balanced, "on the aids."

As you ask for half-pass and then a circle or shoulder-in, and vice versa, the positioning of your aids remains the same (for the bending aids); your weight simply needs to shift to the inside for a "typical" half-pass.

Mistakes in Half-Pass

Mistakes by the Rider

– Acting with the leg aid without preparing the horse for the movement first and causing the horse's hindquarters to outpace his forehand.
– Using the reins incorrectly, causing the horse to lose his bend or slowing him down.
– Leaning back, allowing the chest and shoulders to lag behind the seat and pelvis, or pointing the shoulders in the wrong direction (failing to follow the movement well).

Mistakes by the Horse

– Outpacing his shoulders with his hindquarters.
– Bending too much (you need to adjust the amount of bend with the rein).
– "Dragging" his hindquarters.
– Stepping wide with his inside hind leg (you need to approach the half-pass more gradually, decreasing the angle you're asking for).
– Losing rhythm and regularity (you need to decrease the angle).
– Tilting his head sideways (pay attention to keeping his head straight).
– Losing his bend (practice "swinging" between shoulder-in and half-pass).

Karen Tébar and Fallada, completing a diagonal in half-pass at the canter.

1. Born in the sixth century, and died around 470 BCE; a very great master ... but in another subject.

2. Doctor André, veterinarian, *Mécanique du cheval* [Biomechanics of the Horse], Imprimerie Lavaur, 1950.

3. General Alexis L'Hotte, 1825–1904.

4. Nuno Oliveira, 1925–1989, Portuguese equestrian, known as "the greatest equestrian master of the 20th century ..."

5. Étienne Beudant, 1863–1949, "the miraculous rider" (Decarpentry).

6. See *Placer son cheval* [Positioning the Horse], also by Guillaume Henry, Belin, 2011.

7. Philippe Karl, *Gymnastique du cheval* [Gymnastic Exercises for Horses], Vigot.

8. "Collection" is an arrangement of the horse's body that affects every part of it, and positions each of them with a view to guaranteeing that the horse makes the most of the efforts of his hindquarters. It ensures maximum mobility in all directions, and allows the horse to change speed quickly. It also makes it possible for him to give each of his gaits the maximum elevation possible, at whatever degree the rider chooses to extend or collect the gait, at the rider's request and without delay.

9. "'Collecting' the horse means closing the angle of the head and neck, with the poll remaining the highest point of the latter. 'Collecting' the horse is said to be complete when the head is on the vertical; when the head is behind the vertical, the horse is no longer being gathered toward collection, but rather constrained." (Decarpentry). Contrary to what the term "collecting" might make you picture, it isn't a matter of pulling the head backward toward the body, but rather a matter of pushing the body forward toward the head. See *Placer son cheval* [Positioning the Horse], also by Guillaume Henry, Belin, 2011.

10. *Questions équestres* [Equestrian Matters], General L'Hotte.

11. See *Placer son cheval* [Positioning the Horse], also by Guillaume Henry, Belin, 2011.

12. General Albert Decarpentry, 1878–1956.

13. *Équitation Académique* [Academic Equitation], General Decarpentry.

14. William Cavendish, Duke of Newcastle, 1592–1676.

15. *Équitation Académique* [Academic Equitation], General Decarpentry.

16. Article 401 of the rules of the International Equestrian Federation (FEI).

17. International Equestrian Federation (FEI).

18. I phrase this sentence this way on purpose, to make it clear that if your horse stiffens up, if he "freezes" over the course of your work with him, it's because your exercises aren't relaxing him!

19. General Edmond Wattel, 1878–1957.

20. Lieutenant-Colonel Georges Margot, 1902–1998.

21. Colonel Henri Challan-Belval, 1886–1982.

22. Commander Alexandre Guérin, 1817–1884.

23. *Manuel d'équitation* [Riding Manual], Fédération Française d'Équitation (FFE).

24. Nuno Oliveira.

25. Captain Jacques de Saint-Phalle, 1867–1908.

26. François Baucher, 1796–1873.

27. For a horse "in front of the legs and in the hand," see *Placer son cheval* [Positioning the Horse], also by Guillaume Henry, Belin, 2011.

28. *Manuel d'équitation* [Riding Manual], FFE.

29. See *Placer son cheval* [Positioning the Horse], also by Guillaume Henry, Belin, 2011.

30. A half-turn around the shoulders is also called a reverse half-pirouette, and the full turn is called a reverse pirouette.

31. A half-turn around the haunches is also called a half-pirouette, and the full turn is called a pirouette.

32. Étienne Saurel.

33. François Baucher.

34. The "hand," in riding, begins at the shoulders. This isn't a question of pulling, but of putting "the shoulders at the ends of the arms"—it's the rider's torso that slows down, rather than the hands that pull

back. See *L'Usage des mains* [Using the Hands], also by Guillaume Henry, Belin, 2011.

35. Similarly to the previous note, the "leg" in riding begins at the hips. See *L'Usage des jambes* [Using the Legs], also by Guillaume Henry, Belin, 2011.

36. "Cadence" is a measure of the regularity of the horse's gaits. It's often illustrated with the image of a metronome.

37. Nuno Oliveira.

38. Increase the action of the pelvis in order to accompany the movements of the horse's back, to follow them fully, but *not* to push.

39. Nuno Oliveira.

40. Review the characteristics and common faults of the walk, on page 9-10.

41. At a trot or a canter.

42. Nuno Oliveira.

43. This isn't allowed in competition, but highly recommended in daily work with the horse.

44. Because in this case, typically, the horse will "hollow out" as he tries to slow down, and therefore he won't become round and he won't be on the bit.

45. Which will promote greater engagement, flexibility, and relaxation in the inside hind leg.

46. As mentioned previously, it's always better to work the hands without the legs, and the legs without the hands, using each set of aids independently.

47. Be sure to keep your outside leg back, in this case, so the outside hind leg doesn't swing wide when stopping.

48. See pp 74 and 86.

49. See *S'initier au travail à pied et à longe* [Getting Started with Work In-Hand and on the Longe], also by Guillaume Henry, Belin, 2013.

50. Nuno Oliveira.

51. Étienne Saurel.

52. Except in very special cases, under saddle with a professional and experienced rider.

53. *Manuel d'équitation* [Riding Manual], FFE.

54. Article 406 of the rules of the International Equestrian Federation (FEI).

55. General Decarpentry.

56. *Équitation, la gymnastique du cheval* [Equitation and Gymnastic Exercise for the Horse], Philippe Karl, Vigot, 1980.

57. See *Travail au galop et changement de pied* [Work at Canter and Changes of Lead], also by Guillaume Henry, Belin, 2012.

58. General Decarpentry.

59. And especially no bend to the inside, which would inevitably lead to a young horse positioning himself with his shoulders falling out, his withers low, his back hollow, his croup high ... The whole position would be unnatural, and would make it functionally impossible to straighten or collect the canter.

60. Obviously, the exact opposite is the case for a horse bent to the right.

61. This is why it's better to try to "activate" the gait with this hand, without too much bend.

62. Look for a slower gait, one that can be "broken down" by this hand, without too much bend, to allow your horse to flex his hindquarters.

63. The forelegs then also support the horse's weight equally, symmetrically, and with the same amount of energy ...

64. ... and with lightness, if possible!

65. As explained in number 7 of the "Important Recommendations" in the chapter on "General Considerations" (see page 5).

66. Jacques d'Auvergne, 1729–1798.

67. Who can then, only if it isn't forced, soften and relax your horse.

68. See *Assiette et position* [Seat and Rider Position], also by Guillaume Henry, Belin, 2015.

69. Nuno Oliveira.

70. See page 43-47.

71. A horse who's "on the bit," "on the aids," or "in the hand" is a horse:
– Whose weight on the reins, as a result of the impulsion of the hindquarters, is equal on both sides and confident.
– Who, without resisting with either his neck or his mouth, maintains the contact with the rider's hands and accepts all her aids without difficulty (see *Placer son cheval* [Positioning the Horse], also by Guillaume Henry, Belin, 2011).

72. See number 4 of the "Important Recommendations" in the chapter on "General Considerations" (see page 14).

73 For more on this subject, see *S'initier au travail à pied et à Longe* [Getting Started with Work In-Hand and on the Longe], also Guillaume Henry, Belin, 2013.

74. See page 3.

75. X being the center of the arena, so you are turning around X while maintaining an 8-meter circle.

76. André Jousseaume, 1894–1960.

77. X being the center of the arena, so you are turning around X while maintaining an 8-meter circle.

78. Colonel Henri Challan-Belval.

79. André Jousseaume.

80. X being the center of the arena, so you are turning around X while maintaining an 8-meter circle.

81. See page 43 and following.

82. André Jousseaume.

83. It's the regularity of the gait and the ability of the horse to remain "on the bit" which testify to his degree of flexibility and relaxation in movement; if either is lost, decrease the amount you're asking of him immediately.

84. André Jousseaume.

85. The reverse pirouette (like the pirouette) can be performed with a horse who's bent opposite the direction of the movement (the easiest option for the horse), a horse who's straight, or a horse who's bent in the direction of the movement (the most difficult option for the horse). In the last case, in the reverse pirouette, the horse can be said to be "watching his own haunches coming." Whichever variation you want to try, you need to decide in advance, and maintain the same orientation and bend in the horse throughout the exercise.

86. *Manuel d'équitation* [Riding Manual], FFE.

87. For this "reinforcement" to be effective, your horse needs to be rebalanced first, and typically also needs to be slowed down. You also can't lose sight of the goal of lightness in your aids; if you reinforce a leg aid, it has to be brief, and it can't be the beginning of an escalation where you start pushing harder and harder with your leg.

88. And then at the trot, once the movement no longer poses any difficulty at the walk and can be done in a state of relaxation and lightness.

89. It is true that the horse's movement can be considered a shoulder-in if he's counter-bent and moving without crossing his hind legs, and a leg-yield if he's straight and is crossing his hind legs.

90. From the rules of the International Equestrian Federation (FEI).

91. *Manuel d'équitation et de dressage* [Equitation and Dressage Manual], Étienne Saurel.

92. François Robichon de La Guérinière, 1688–1751.

93. Which corresponds to the "strengthening" phase of the canter, and to a horse in collection.

94. Gustave Le Bon, 1841–1913.

95. See drawing on page 75.

96. General Decarpentry.

97. That is, including and returning to a circle between each exercise.

98. General Decarpentry.

99. James Fillis, 1834–1913, quoted by Étienne Saurel in *Pratique de l'équitation d'après les maîtres français* [The Practice of Riding, According to the French Masters].

100. The "swing" referred to here is not in your upper body; you're "swinging" between your inside and outside aids.

101. It's a mistake for the hips to outpace or precede the shoulders; in half-pass, the shoulders should slightly precede the hips.

Bibliography

Albrecht, Kurt, *Les Dogmes de l'art* équestre [The Dogmas of Equestrian Art], Paris, Crépin-Leblond, 1985.

Auvinet, Bernard, and Estrade, Murielle, *La Santé du cavalier, Conseils pratiques pour une* équitation *sans risque* [The Horseman's Health: Practical Advice for Risk-Free Riding], Paris, Chiron, 1998.

Bacharach, René, *Réponses* équestres [Equestrian Answers], Lausanne, Favre-Caracole, 1986.

Baucher, Francois, *Dictionnaire raisonné d'équitation* [Comprehensive Dictionary of Riding], Paris, Émile Hazan, 1966.

Method of Equitation Based on New Principles, Foundation for the Equestrian Arts, 2017.

Beudant, Étienne, *Main sans jambes ...* [Hand Without Legs ...] Lyon, Editions de la Guillotière, 1945.

Vallerine, le testament d'un écuyer [Vallerine: The Testament of a Horseman], Paris, Lausanne, Favre, 2005.

Bragança, Dom Diogo (de), *Dressage in the French Tradition*, Xenophon Press, 2012.

Challan-Belval (Colonel), *Dressage* [Dressage], Paris, Émile Hazan, 1964.

Chiris, Bernard, *L'Art de monter à cheval* [The Art of Riding], Paris, Belin, 2003.

Chambry, Pierre, *Allures et Sentiment* [Gaits and Feel], Paris, Maloine, 1990.

Decarpentry (General),

Piaffe and Passage, released in a single volume along with *The Spanish Riding School in Vienna*, Xenophon Press, 2013.

Academic Equitation, Trafalgar Square Books, 2012.

La Méthode de Haute École de Raabe [The Methods of the High School of Raabe], Berger-Levrault, 1957, republished by Paris, Émile Hazan, 1980.

Conseils à un jeune cavalier [Advice to a Young Rider (exact title: Advice from General Decarpentry to a Young Horseman: Notes on Equestrian Instruction and Dressage Theory)], collected by Colonel Xavier Lesage, presented and edited by General Durand, Paris, Lausanne, Favre, 2004.

Faverot de Kerbrech (General), *Methodical Dressage of the Riding Horse*, released in a single volume along with *Dressage of the Outdoor Horse*, Xenophon Press, 2015.

FFE/DNSE, *Les* Épreuves *de dressage: notes d'orientation à l'intention des cavaliers et des juges* [Dressage Tests: Notes of Guidance Intended for Riders and Judges], Paris, Lavauzelle, 1991.

FFSE, *Manuel d'équitation* [Riding Manual], Paris, Lavauzelle, 1968.

Fillis, James,

Principles of Dressage and Equitation, Xenophon Press, 2018.

Journal de dressage [Journal of Dressage], Paris, 1903.

Règlement pour le dressage du cheval d'armes [Regulations for the Dressage Training of the Military Horse], Loudun, PSR, 2003.

Force, Jean-Luc, *Enseigner l'équitation: manuel à l'usage des enseignants et de leurs cavaliers* [Teaching Horseback Riding: Manual for Trainers and Riders], Paris, Lavauzelle, 2001.

Franconi, Victor, *Le Cavalier et l'Écuyer* [The Rider and the Horseman], Paris, J.-. Square, 1991.

Gérard, André, *Les Maîtres de l'équitation classique* [The Masters of Classical Riding], Verviers, Arts Library, 1974.

Henriquet, Michel, *Comportement et Dressage* [Behavior and Dressage], Paris, Belin, 2009.

Gymnase et Dressage [Gymnasium and Dressage], Paris, Maloine, 1991.

30 Years with Master Nuno Oliveira: Correspondence, Photographs, and Notes, Xenophon Press, 2011.

Le Débourrage du cheval [Breaking in the Horse], Strasbourg, Cavalcade, 1999.

Le travail à pied [Work on the Ground], Strasbourg, Cavalcade, 1999.

Karl, Philippe, *Dérives du dressage moderne, recherche d'une alternative classique* [Derivations of Modern Dressage (and the) Search for a Classical Alternative],

Paris, Vigot, 2022.

Une certaine idée du dressage [A Certain Idea of Dressage], Paris, Belin, 2006.

L'Emploi des longues rênes [Using Long Reins], Paris, Belin, 2004.

Équitation: la gymnastique du cheval [Equitation: Gymnastic Exercises for the Horse], Paris, Vigot, 1980.

L'Hotte, Alexis (General), *Equestrian Questions*, released in a single volume along with *The Quest for Lightness in Equitation*, Xenophon Press, 2021.

Licart (Commander), *Comment apprendre à monter à cheval* [How to Learn to Ride a Horse], Paris, Delmas, 1976.

Équitation raisonnée [Reasoned Riding], Paris, Delmas, 1972.

Perfectionnement équestre [Equestrian Improvement], Paris, Delmas, 1972.

Müseler, Wilhelm, *Riding Logic*, Trafalgar Square Books, 2021.

Oliveira, Nuno, *Equestrian Art: The Collected Later Works*, Xenophon Press, 2022.

Podhajsky, Alois, *L'Équitation* [Horseback Riding], Paris, Odège, 1968.

Racinet, Jean-Claude, *Racinet Explains Baucher*, Xenophon Press, 2014.

Saurel, Étienne, *Pratique de l'équitation d'après les maîtres français* [The Practice of Riding, According to the French Masters], Paris, Flammarion, 1964.

Sévy L. de, *Assiette, Allures, et Réactions* [The Seat, the Gaits, and the Responses of the Horse], Paris, Chapelot, 1920.

Les Allures, le Cavalier [The Gaits and the Rider], Paris, Librairies Legoupy and Chapelot, 1919.

Steinbrecht, Gustav, *The Gymnasium of the Horse*, Xenophon Press, 2014.

Swift, Sally, *Centered Riding*, Trafalgar Square Books, 1985.

Journals

Articles published in *Cheval Magazine* [Horse Magazine].

Boisson, Jean-Jacques, "Le Fonctionnement du cavalier: vaste débat" [The Performance of the Rider: A Vast Debate], *L'Équitation*, issue 16, p. 17.

Galloux, Bieau, Jeddi, Auvinet, Lacouture, "Le Fonctionnement du cavalier sur le plat: adaptation biomécanique du cavalier à cheval, au trot et au galop" [The Performance of the Rider on the Flat: Biomechanical Adaptation of the Rider on Horseback, at Trot and at Canter], *L'Équitation*, issue 16, p. 18-22.

Girard, Jean-Franck,

"Les Attitudes et fonctionnements du cavalier de dressage" [The Bearing and Performance of the Dressage Rider], *L'Équitation*, issue 16, p. 13-16.

"Les Attitudes et fonctionnements du cavalier de dressage" [The Bearing and Performance of the Dressage Rider], *L'Équitation*, issue 17, p. 34-40.

"Les Attitudes et fonctionnements du cavalier de dressage" [The Bearing and Performance of the Dressage Rider], *L'Équitation*, issue 18, p. 34-37

Acknowledgments

Some of the elements of this book are based on data sheets created by Alain Francqueville.

May he find here an expression of all my gratitude for his help. Thank you also to Georges Fizet from Haras de Fleurville for his proofreading and editorial comments.

The publisher would like to thank all the people appearing in the photographs this book contains.